Those Were The Days!

Circa 1940 "Large Letter" novelty postcard

Greetings from Maine...Greetings to Maine

Drive-Ins, Dance Halls, Fried Clams, Summer & Maine

Those Were The Days!

by Will Anderson

Anderson & Sons' Publishing Co.
34 Park Street
Bath, Maine 04530
(207) 442-7459

A Maine-Owned and Operated Company Since 1987

Other Books by Will Anderson

Beers, Breweries & Breweriana (1969)
The Beer Book (1973)
The Beer Poster Book (1977)
Beer, New England (1988)
New England Roadside Delights (1989)
Mid-Atlantic Roadside Delights (1991)
Was Baseball Really Invented In Maine? (1992)
Good Old Maine (1993)
More Good Old Maine (1995)
The Great State Of Maine Beer Book (1996)
Where Have You Gone, Starlight Cafe? (1998)
You Auto See Maine (1999)
Lost Diners And Roadside Restaurants Of New England And New York (2001)

Will Anderson 1940-

1. Maine 2. Drive-In Theatres 3. Popular Culture
ISBN 1-893804-02-X

Studio Photography by A. & J. DuBois Commercial Photography, Lewiston, Maine · Artwork on pages 134 and 148 by Dick Hubsch, Carmel, New York · Art Direction and Production by Tim Gagnon, Lewiston, Maine · Printed by Spectrum Printing and Graphics, Auburn, Maine · Cover Lamination by New England Finishing, Holyoke, Massachusetts · Bound by Optimum Bindery Services of New England, Nashua, New Hampshire · Front Cover Concept by Dick Hubsch, Carmel, New York · Front Cover Art by John Bowdren, Pownal, Maine

TABLE OF CONTENTS

ACKNOWLEDGEMENTS

In the search for both information and graphic material for THOSE WERE THE DAYS! I had the assistance of several score of people from all across Maine and beyond. Many of these good people are included in the book's text. Those not included there are included here. THANKS to you all. And SPECIAL THANKS to Peter C. Bachelder of Ellsworth for his very generous loan of a number of much-appreciated postcard images used in the book.

Edward Barrett, City of Bangor, Bangor, Maine • Kathie Barrie, Portland Public Library, Portland, Maine • Dorothy A. Blanchard, Newcastle, Maine • Jim Brown, City of Presque Isle, Presque Isle, Maine • Christy Coombs, Bangor Public Library, Bangor, Maine • Anne Cough, Maine State Library, Augusta, Maine • Richard Day, Damariscotta Historical Society, Damariscotta, Maine • Elie R. Duguay, Livermore Falls, Maine • Andrea Dyer , Presque Isle Historical Society, Presque Isle, Maine • Arthur Faucher, Town of Madawaska, Madawaska, Maine • Priscilla Gallant, Old Orchard Beach Historical Society, Old Orchard Beach, Maine • Marcia Goodwin, Springvale Public Library, Springvale, Maine • Rosella A. Loveitt, South Portland Historical Society, South Portland, Maine • Susan Luse, Patten Free Library, Bath, Maine • Myrtle McKenna, Rumford Historical Society, Rumford, Maine • Ralph C. Monroe, Milo Historical Society, Milo, Maine • Kristin Morris, Patten Free Library, Bath, Maine • Marlene Parent, Springvale Public Library, Springvale, Maine • Guy Reed, Woolwich, Maine • Richard M. Riegel, Cincinnati, Ohio • Randy Roberts, Thomaston, Maine • Myra Rosenbaum, Charles M. Bailey Public Library, Winthrop, Maine • Christine Small, East Machias, Maine • Virginia S. Spiller, Old York Historical Society, York, Maine • Sarah W. Steinman, Yarmouth Chamber of Commerce, Yarmouth, Maine • Theresa Troegner, University of Southern Maine, Portland, Maine

**To my granddaughters, Kelsey and Lindy Hop (a.k.a. Lindsey)…
May you always treasure the beauty and wonder of a book.**

Photo, February 2002. That's Lindsey on the left and Kelsey on the right.

Riding the Rides
Circa 1950
postcard view

Courting
Circa 1950
comic postcard

Sightseeing
Circa 1945
postcard view

This book came into being because of a desire to highlight the joys of that best of all Maine seasons, summertime. Past and present. And specifically pop culture types of joy. Past and present. As the idea bloomed and grew I asked friends and neighbors what they, through the years, most enjoyed about summer. "Warmth" came in number one, followed by a whole raft of favorite activities. Going to the beach ranked high. So did drives in the country, picnics, and either participating in or watching a summer sport: baseball, softball, golf, etc. Even horseshoes. Hiking, sailing, and all of the other "doings" portrayed over these several pages via period postcards and other ephemera garnered votes as well.

Of all these pastimes there were three that stood out for me. The first was dancing. I've long enjoyed "cutting a rug" or two but I've always thought of dancing as a year around activity. Not so in Maine in "the good old days." Through the 1920s, 1930s, 1940s, and even into the 1950s, dancing was often

Preface

a summer joy in many locales. Most dances were held in large, often downright cavernous, dance halls. Many of these halls weren't heated. Even if they were, management ofttimes still preferred the comfort of summer tourists, their dancing shoes, their paid admissions. What these halls lacked in months of operation, however, they made up with summer nights in operation. It seemed as if there were a band playing somewhere every eve. And we are talking a band; even an orchestra. The idea of a disc jockey would have been almost abhorrent.

Joy Number Two

Standout summertime fun activity number two was going to the drive-in movie theatre. Lights out at dusk and popcorn, hamburgers, and French fries while taking in a double feature starring the likes of Jack Palance, Rhonda Fleming, Sterling Hayden, Ida Lupino, and so often, or so it seemed, Audie Murphy. Park your Chevy Belair or your Hudson Hornet where

Hanging Out
Circa 1950
comic postcard

Motoring About
Circa 1915
comic postcard

Fishing (and Fabricating?)
Circa 1945
comic postcard

9

Hitting the Water
Circa 1940 greeting
card graphic

Watching a Ballgame
Portland Pilots' "Official
Program and Score
Card," 1949

you wanted: toward the back if you really didn't come to watch what was on the big screen; toward the front if you came with the kiddies all decked out in their pajamas for what was, in so many ways, the perfect family night out.

And Fried Clams Make Three

Our last sweet, sweet summertime treat is eating. While once-seasonal goodies as corn on the cob and ice cream are now available year around they seem to taste far better when it's 85° than when it's 35°. Ditto for hamburgers, cheeseburgers, hot dogs… and fried clams. And it was fried clams that most excited the people with whom I spoke. I'm not saying they drooled at the mouth, but there certainly was many a happy smile at the very thought of glomming down a serving or two of those crispy crustaceans. So fried clams it is with respect to the eating aspect of the joys of a Maine summer. Eat hearty.

Enjoy your trip down Maine drive-in, dance hall, fried clam lane.

Preface

A pair of road maps from when they were both beautiful and were given away free. The Shell map is from 1932; the Tydol from the late 1940s

LET'S DANCE:
MAINE'S DANCE HALL HERITAGE

I've begun this ode to dance halls with the 1920s because it was in the 1920s that dance halls really started to bloom in Maine. And, in keeping with the book's theme of summertime yesterdays, I did my best to focus on open-for-the-summer-only dance halls and pavilions. Lastly, I concentrated on establishments that were conceived and constructed primarily for dancing purposes. Commercial dancing establishments. With that in mind, I have excluded the lion's share of American Legion and VFW halls, granges, hotels, town halls and the like.

Dance Halls

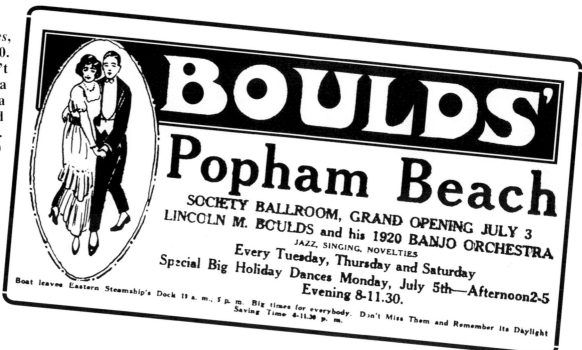

THE 1920s

The Roaring Twenties did not skip Maine. Not by a long shot. Not when it came to dancing. By my best estimation there were well over 100 assorted dance halls, pavilions, and "casinos" (plus granges, town halls, Odd Fellows, etc.) that regularly held dances during "the season" in that decade of Lucky Lindy, the Babe, and Warren G. Harding. Following is a good sampling of those that appeared to be the most successful.

At the start of the decade, Peaks Island was rolling with the Peaks Island Pavilion, featuring dancing every night in "A Place Of Refinement." Then there was Dayburn Casino, at Trefethens Landing (also on Peaks). "Bring your girl to the coolest and finest dance hall in Maine," ran its ads. In Lewiston there was the Mystic Ballroom, with music by the Mystic Famous Orchestra and an admission fee of 40¢. Winthrop's legendary Island Park had dancing four nights a week plus a Special Chicken Dinner in the event you felt more like eating than dancing. Popham Beach was home to Boulds' Popham Beach Society Ballroom, with

Ad, *The Ariel*, publication of East Maine Conference Seminary, Bucksport, June 1922. To be taken for "old J.D. himself" was quite the compliment in 1922, for "J.D." was none other than John D. Rockefeller, the man with more money than any other man in the world at the time.

> **UNGUARDED WOMEN**
> It was the era of the Charleston, flappers, bootleg booze, jazz, F. Scott Fitzgerald… and wild women. A popular movie of the day (1924) was UNGUARDED WOMEN. Billed as "A Story Of A Modern Jazz-Wild Girl And A Man's Unselfish Attempt To Reform Her," it starred Bebe Daniels as "The Girl" and Richard Dix as "The Man."

Lincoln M. Boulds and his 1920 Banjo Orchestra furnishing the music every Tuesday, Thursday, and Saturday evening. Rockland pitched in with its Arcade Dance Hall. Their slogan: "Another Good Time." And Houlton had its Crescent Park. In fact, Crescent Park's season opener in 1921 was good enough for front page news in the *Houlton Times*. "All roads led to Crescent Park Wednesday when the season's activities were started in full swing with a big dance," noted the *Times'* edition of June 1st, adding "The weather was all that could be desired and one of the largest crowds ever seen at this pleasant resort were (sic) present."

Succeeding years saw Sebenoa Hall, in Woolwich, with the Princess Manhattan Colored Orchestra, a six-piece combo from New York City, providing the music. On Monday nights, no less. In ads in *The Bangor Daily News*, the Ja-Mo-Ka Orchestra promised "Big Dancing Parties" all along their tour of the North Country. From Mars Hill,

Continued on page 18

Postcard view, circa 1940

362 Good Times   Wells Beach Maine

ISLAND LEDGE CASINO
WELLS

Although never of the calibre of Old Orchard Beach, Wells Beach nevertheless reached for the big time with its Island Ledge Casino. The dream of a man named John M. Davis, Island Ledge was erected in 1915 for the then hefty sum of $20,000. Akin to a number of other beachside endeavors, it was a "one stop" entertainment mecca. As described on the address side of the postcard to the lower right, Island Ledge consisted of "a moving picture theatre, high class dance hall, billiard and pool rooms, bowling alleys, ice cream parlor and restaurant." Why go anywhere else?

Dance Halls

ISLAND LEDGE CASINO, WELLS BEACH, ME.

PICTURES   DANCING

TURNER CENTRE ICE CREAM   SOFT DRINKS   CANDIES-TOYS   ISLAND LEDGE CASINO   DANCING   MOVING PICTURES   BOWLING

Postcard view, circa 1915

Postcard view, circa 1920

During the summer season there was dancing at the Casino on Tuesday, Thursday, and Saturday evenings; movies every other night and afternoons, too. During the winter season the Casino was closed. Movie theatre kingpin E.M. Loew bought the Island Ledge in the 1930s. A name change, to Wells Beach Casino and Theatre, was effected in 1943. In 1979 local restaurateurs Vander Forbes, Sr. and Jr. purchased the venerable complex. After seven years of upkeep the Forbes decided to junk the longtime landmark. It was leveled in the fall of 1986. On the site now is the Forbes Wells Beach Resort.

PICTURES   DANCING   ISLAND LEDGE CASINO

BOWLING ALLEY POOL ROOM

ISLAND LEDGE CASINO, J. M. DAVIS, PROP., WELLS BEACH, ME.

Joke, *The Oracle*, the publication of Edward Little High School, Auburn, 1927

Joe: "Where's the surgeon tonight?"
Moe: "He went to a dance."
Joe: "Well, the old cut-up!"

Corny jokes are timeless. Here's one from 1927 that just might have you in stitches. Or at least make you smile.

Continued from page 15

Houlton, and Fort Fairfield to Presque Isle, Ashland, and Caribou there certainly were few Aroostook hot spots that Ja-Mo-Ka missed. Then there was the Bear Pond Park Pavilion in North Turner, Pinkham's Hall in East Holden, the Thistle in Searsport, the Roseland Ball Room in Dexter, the Skylight Pavilion in Augusta, the Casino in Bar Harbor, and Camp Benson - billed as "The Ballroom On The Lake" - in Newport. The Milo Pavilion's ads read "The Milo Pavilion Speaks for Itself," while Hartwell's Landing, on Pleasant Lake in Stetson, offered Shorey's All-Singing Orchestra plus "Up-to-date Dances." And the Crescent Ballroom, in Union, rang out that it was "Maine's Largest Ball Room." With a capacity of 1,500 couples, it probably was. Then there was Oakland Park, the "Famous Picnic Resort and Pleasure Paradise" in Rockport, where one could dance under 1000 mirrors in "Maine's Most Marvelous Moonlit Ball Room."

Leclair's Dance Pavilion, at Gurnet Bridge (outside of

Dance Halls

Brunswick), promised a swell time from 8:30 to 11:45 every Wednesday and Saturday on "The best dancing floor in the State." Not to be outdone, Island Park billed itself as the "New" Island Park, "The Home Of Clean Dancing." And Auburn kicked in with the Oakdale Pavilion, located on the State Road in the vicinity of Danville Junction. Admission was 50¢ for the men; 30¢ for the ladies.

In addition to their Peaks Island choices, Portland highsteppers could select from the Jack O' Lantern ("Fanned by Ocean Breezes") in South Portland, the Riverside Pavilion (where Al Sherlock and his Snappy Syncopators held forth), and the Sunset Ballroom at the monumental Riverton Park.

The list of old and new favorites continued through the Twenties. Sometimes you had to love the hyperbole. There was, for example, the Flower Garden, in Wayne, which quoted Oliver Wendell Holmes in its ads while proclaiming itself "Maine's Most Popular Dance Center." Then there was Portland's Riverside Pavilion. Its claim: "The wonderful floor and charming music and refined patronage assures you of a delightfully social evening." Not to be overlooked was the Gray Road Inn, on the Portland-Auburn road ("The Ballroom Beautiful"), and the Gem Ballroom, on Peaks Island ("Where The 'Classy' Girls and Boys Meet").

And you had to admire - if not love - the stamina of the dancing crowd. Midnight - *starting at midnight* - dances were far from uncommon. Often called Frolics, they were a regular feature heading into Decoration Day, July 4th, and Labor Day. "Put The BANG in BANGOR" headlined a 4th of July ad for the Big Special Holiday Dance that lasted 'til 4:00 A.M. at Bangor's elegant Chateau, while 50¢ admitted you to Oakdale Pavilion's big Labor Day Morning Dance And Frolic. Or how about the Long Beach Sabattus Dance Pavilion's Labor Day morning gala, with music provided by the Ritz Radio Ramblers Orchestra from 12:30 to 6:30? The Palace and the Pier, both in Old Orchard, Lewiston's Beacon Ballroom, and the Gray Road Inn - with "The Snappiest Band in Maine," Clate Whittier and His Melody Kings, providing the sounds - held all-night Labor Day eve celebrations as well, while the Naples Casino and Rice's Beach Pavilion did likewise for the 4th of July. Fireworks, confetti, streamers, noisemakers: all were generally aplenty, too. The Riverside Pavilion, however, went a step further for their Labor Day extravaganza: they held a Dancing & Corn Roast. "Come, dance and be merry on the best floor in Portland" ran their ads, adding "Free corn well buttered."

Maine and dancing and the 1920s are perhaps best summed up by an event that occurred the evening of August 31st, 1929. A fire broke out at Island Park. Eighteen persons, including half of Lionel Doucette & His 8 Stars band, were taken to Augusta General for treatment. "Not to be cheated out of their evening's enjoyment, however," the *Portland Sunday Telegram* reported in its September 1st front-page headline story, "those who escaped a scorching" just shifted gears to a nearby unscathed dance pavilion… and kept on dancing.

Dance Halls

Dancing far into the night (morning?) was a longtime eve of Decoration Day/the Fourth of July/Labor Day tradition. This ad for Newport's Roseland and Camp Benson is from *The Bangor Daily News* of July 2, 1925.

A rather delightful drawing from the pen of one Helen McDonald for the June, 1937 edition of *The Chiefton*, the magazine of the Bangor School of Commerce, Bangor.

Dance Halls

THE 1930s

The 1930s saw the inception of the term "Dine and Dance." In some instances the term resulted from a dance hall adding a full or fuller menu. The venerable Gray Road Inn, located on the Lewiston-Portland road, was an example of this. The Gray Road began using the term in May 1930. In most cases, however, the term was utilized by established restaurants in an attempt to garner some of the considerable dance hall crowd business. Examples included the Links Inn, in Hampden; the Oriental Restaurant, in Lewiston; Bangor's Atlantic Restaurant and Night Garden; the Royal Restaurant (which touted "The Finest Dining Room East of Boston"), also in Lewiston; and Phil's Place, on the Lewiston road in Winthrop. All offered food and at least some sort of a band and dance floor.

July of 1933 also saw the return of "happy days." Beer - legal beer! - came back on the scene after an absence, in Maine, of over 80 years. Some dance pavilion proprietors avoided the beer bandwagon. Others jumped aboard. Among those who welcomed the amber liquid were Oakdale Gardens, in Auburn; Pulsifer's Ballroom, at Minot Corner; the Gray Road Inn, still on the Lewiston-Portland road; the Pirate's Den, in Norway; and Lucerne-

Circa 1935 "Dine and Dance" matchbook cover art

Continued on page 28

OLD ORCHARD BEACH

Just about everybody, it seemed, went to Old Orchard Beach. They came by auto. By bus. By train. They came to swim, to enjoy the amusements, to eat… and to dance. On any given summertime evening the odds are that O.O.B. was jumping.

Ad, *Bath Daily Times,*
July 9, 1930

Dance Halls

PALACE BALL ROOM, OLD ORCHARD BEACH, MAINE.

PALACE BALLROOM

"All Roads Lead To The Palace Ballroom" read a summer 1927 ad. The ad was about right.

PALACE BALL ROOM BUILDING, CAPACITY 4,000. LARGEST IN NEW ENGLAND.

OLD ORCHARD BEACH, MAINE.

Postcard views, all circa 1940. The interior view is courtesy of Dan Blaney, Old Orchard Beach.

Amusement Center at Night, Old Orchard Beach, Maine

Built by a businessman named Charles Usen in 1924, the Palace played host to hundreds of big name acts and thousands of dancing couples in its 43 years of existence.

THE PIER

For the better part of four decades the Pier Casino was one of America's dance band hot spots. As worded so well by Peter D. Bachelder in his splendid 1998 book, THE GREAT STEEL PIER: "From the late 1920s well into the 1950s, literally every big-name touring ensemble made the Old Orchard Beach Pier Casino a 'must stop' on its hectic itinerary of one-night stands. Among the favorites were: Count Basie, Duke Ellington, Cab Calloway, Louis Armstrong, Benny Goodman, Guy Lombardo, Sammy Kaye, Tommy and Jimmy Dorsey, and Glenn Miller."

Postcard view, circa 1945. See if you can find the Pier Casino and the Palace Ballroom. They're both here in this quite magnificent aerial shot.

Dance Halls

View of the Pier at Old Orchard Beach, Maine — D-36

Postcard view, circa 1940. The Pier had as its slogan "Dance O'er The Waves." It was true.

THE PIER FROM OLD ORCHARD STREET, OLD ORCHARD BEACH, MAINE

Postcard view, circa 1935.

"I'll always remember the Pier one real warm July night (in 1939). There were three of us from Bath. We'd hitchhiked over. The place was so crowded: Glenn Miller and his Orchestra were playing. It was so crowded you couldn't dance, as big as the dance floor was. So we said to ourselves, 'We came here to dance, not just watch the band.' We went outside and there we met three young girls who were standing there talking. I'll never forget what a beautiful night it was: the full moon and with a sub-tropical breeze blowing. We danced (with the three girls) on the pier. And before long other people began moving out on the pier to dance, too. It got really crowded there, too. We danced 'til 1:00. Then we got a ride from the dance hall to Freeport. By that time it was getting late. We thumbed awhile. There were a few cars, but none of them stopped. So we went into the hayloft of a barn that was on the side of the road and slept there. When we got back on the road the next morning, boy, were we a mess. Hayseed all over us. But it was all worth it. We laughed about it for years."

Reid Perkins, 81, Bath
October 24, 2000

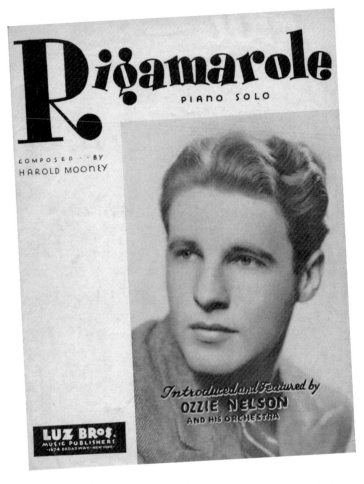

Sheet music cover, 1935. Can you guess who this is? A hint: both of his sons looked a lot like he did. He was a bandleader of considerable renown; married his vocalist; went on to star in his own top radio show and then his own top tv show. His name: Ozzie Nelson. And he and his vocalist and wife-to-be, Harriet Hilliard, played the Dreamwood Ballroom in Bar Harbor on June 29, 1934. In its ads Dreamwood billed Harriet as "Radio's Most Beautiful Songbird."

Continued from page 23

In-Maine, located southeast of Bangor. The Beach Inn, on Long Beach in Sabattus, added a pair of exclamation marks - as in "BEER!!" - in their ads, while Bangor's Atlantic Restaurant and Night Garden heralded "Dancing," "Delightful Menu," and "4 Cold Friends:" Schlitz, Pabst Blue Ribbon and Trommer's by the bottle, and Goldenrod (a shortlived Brooklyn brew) on draught. Although not a dance hot spot, Ye Old Tavern Restaurant, located on Exchange Street in Maine's Queen City, outdid them all. It offered free beer with each order of a chicken dinner. And the chicken dinner was only 50¢ to begin with.

Whether dance patrons, in those golden years before WWII, liked their beer or not was a matter of personal choice. Not so, however, when it came to the names of the bandstand orchestras they danced to. You *had* to like those names. After all, they were "cool."

28

Dance Halls

Name That Band

The names of the bands and orchestras that got folks up and waltzing and fox trotting and Lindy hopping from Kittery to Fort Kent in those golden years before World War II sound dated - even "quaint" - now. But they were "cool" then. And often selected to give an air of "importance." Or to imply - be it true or not - that the band's members were from some far off, exotic place. Like Pennsylvania or Carolina or Georgia. Here's a rundown (with the dance hall in which they played) of some favorites of mine. Let's start with **Kermit Collins & His Bostonians** (Sylvester's Pavilion, Durham); the **Colonial Serenaders** (The Pier, Old Orchard); **Saxie Dyer & His Carolinians** (Lake Beach Pavilion, Sabattus); **Al Lombardo & His Twelve Aristocrats** (Thomas' Point Pavilion, Brunswick); and **Perley Reynolds & His Commanders** (Mineral Spring Pavilion, Blue Hill).

Like alliteration? There was the **Alabama Aces** (the Jack O' Lantern, billed as "Maine's First and Only Combined Indoor and Outdoor Ball Room," in South Portland); **Harry Hicks & His Carolinians** (Bridge Hall, Winnegance… home of the Human Eel Dance); **Piper Manning & His Haywire Haylofters** (at the Hayloft, in Naples); and **Lennie Lizotte & His Silver Slipper Club Orchestra** (Crystal Ballroom, Dover-Foxcroft).

And who could forget **Shorty Bowen's Highland Merrymakers** (Twilight Pavilion, Hermon Pond); **Davidson's Troubadours** (Tacoma Lakes, Litchfield); the **Philharmonic Serenaders** (Palace Ballroom, Old Orchard); **Lloyd Rafnell & His Georgians** (Crescent Lake Pavilion, Webbs Mills); **Dave Hatch and his Virginians** (Oakland Park, Rockport); the **Knightkappers Orchestra** (General Warren Lobster House, Kittery, which advertised "New England's Finest Crystal-Cool Dance Floor"); and **Forest Smith and his Serenaders** (Alexander's Pavilion, North Belgrade).

And For Good Measure

Other notable dance spots in operation at one time or another during the thirties included the Hillside Pavilion (Stockton Springs); Paradise Pavilion (Bangor); Riverside Pavilion (Portland); Monitor Hall (Orono); the Anchorage (Harrison); Sim's Danceland (Freeport); Wildwood (Steep Falls); Blue Moon Inn (Sabattus); Silver Slipper Club (Auburn); White Horse Inn (Poland Springs); Ludwig's Casino (Richmond); Hall's Pavilion (East Livermore); Island Park (Winthrop); Highland Grove (Standish); Freelove's Pavilion (North Bridgton); Gem Ball Room (Peaks Island); Whip-O-Will (Orland); Villa Vaughn (Pushaw Lake); the Old Grist Mill (Lagrange); Seaboard Club (Bucksport); Prairie Pavilion (home of Lewis Stone & His Down East LumberJacks, Brownville); Camp Benson Park (Newport); Midway Pavilion (Orono); the Flower Garden (Wayne); Paul's Arena (Maple Grove); Joe Chabot's Place (Livermore Falls); Lakeside Landing (Pushaw Lake), Tracy's Barn Dance (Sidney); Tacoma Lakes Pavilion (Litchfield); Clary Lake Casino (Jefferson); the Hilltop Pavilion (Knox); Indian Lake Pavilion (East Machias); the Bar-L (Newport); Lakeside (Lincoln); and the elegantly-named Silver Slipper Ball Room (Milford).

The most popular name was "Dreamwood." There were at least three - almost certainly not related - in operation during the decade. There was Dreamwood #1, in Bar Harbor; Dreamwood #2, in Hampden; Dreamwood #3, in Mattawamkeag. Number three boasted: "Wonderful Floor - Plenty of Room - Real Cool Hall."

You get the idea. There was a tremendous number of places - and far flung places - where one could "cut a rug" on a summer's night. A few spots even continued that holiday tradition, the starting-at-midnight gala. Among those spots, closing out Labor Day weekend 1939, were Lakehurst (Damariscotta), Torrey Hill Barn (North Turner), the Pier (Old

Dance Halls

Orchard), Wildwood (Steep Falls), the everpresent Gray Road Inn, the Riverside Pavilion (New Gloucester), and the Crescent Lake Pavilion (Webbs Mills). Then there was the Crystal Ballroom (Dover-Foxcroft), Mineral Springs Ballroom (Blue Hill), the Bar-L (Newport), Lakeside Pavilion (Lincoln), the New Gypsy (Bucksport), and the Dreamland Pavilion (Mattawamkeag). All ran their respective shindigs from midnight to 4:00 AM. Except for the Torrey Hill Barn. It promised music and merriment "to the wee hours in the morning."

As the old saying goes: "How are you going to keep 'em down on the farm after they've seen North Turner?"

DANCE HALL

In the 1930s and 1940s dance halls were so in vogue there was even a movie entitled DANCE HALL. Released in 1941, it starred Carol Landis and Cesar Romero in a typical romantic musical of the day: Romero owns a dance hall; Landis works there; the two fall in love.

GORDON HOWE AND HIS ORCHESTRA

Born in Richmond in 1916, Gordon Howe began playing piano at age six and grew up to be the dean of Maine bandleaders. What he wanted to be, however, was a ballplayer. He was a southpaw pitcher for the old Richmond High; good, but not good enough to go any further.

So Gordon embraced his second love, music, forming his own band, Gordon Howe and the Blue Romancers, in 1933. "It (the name) just sounded intriguing," he said in an October 2000 interview at his Richmond home.

Starting with a six-piece assemblage, Gordon went on to eight, then fourteen. He dropped "the Blue Romancers," circa 1940, in favor of the more fashionable "Gordon Howe and his Orchestra." By the late 1940s Gordon was a fixture at such storied dance halls as Lakeview Pavilion, in South China; Oakland Park, in Rockport; and Island Park, in Winthrop. "They were all nice, nice ballrooms," he fondly recalls. Most requested songs were Glenn Miller's *In The Mood* and *String of Pearls*, Benny

Dance Halls

Goodman's *Let's Dance*, and Artie Shaw's *Begin The Beguine*. "I had a cornet player who could really cut it on that song," Gordon smiles. Gordon played - with less frequency as he and his band members got older and rock and roll more popular - through the 1980s; even playing one last gig at the Atrium in Brunswick in 1995. How does he sum up over sixty years of making music? "I just loved it all," he beams.

Gordon at the mike, Lakeview, 1947. The Blue Romancers' first paying job, at Pownalborough Town Hall in 1934, didn't pay very much. "We were paid all of $7.50... to be split six ways," he recalls with a chortle all these years later. Photo courtesy of Gordon Howe, Richmond.

Gordon Howe and his Orchestra at the Lakeview, in South China, in 1947, That's Gordon on the piano; his then-wife and vocalist, Rena, on the right. Photo courtesy of Russell Ring, Union.

THE 1940s

The 1940s started, dancingwise, with a vengeance. Music was in the air. So were dance hall improvements and renovations. Carmel's Auto Rest Park ballyhooed a new, larger, 5,000 square foot dance floor plus parking for over 500 cars. "The Most Beautiful Summer Dance Hall in Maine," proclaimed Auto Rest's management. Other dance spots in the Bangor area included the Roseland Ballroom ("Best Music and Dance Floor in Bangor"); Briggs' Pavilion, at Pea Cove; the Old Grist Mill, in Lagrange; the Crystal Ballroom, in Dover-Foxcroft; the Whip-O-Will, in Orland (which featured, as well, rollerskating on Sunday afternoon and evening); Newport's venerable Bar-L; the Hillside Pavilion, in Stockton Springs; Luckey Landing, on Pushaw Lake (also newly enlarged and which claimed "Largest Dance Floor In Northeastern Maine," plus dancing to "That All Collegiate Band," the Bates Bobcats); Islehurst in Trenton; the Pleasant Lake Pavilion, in Stetson; Lakeside Hall, in Lincoln (where you could skate and then dance); and Dreamwood, located in Hampden and also boasting a newly enlarged -

Continued on page 37

WARD SHAW, AND PERLEY REYNOLDS AND HIS COMMANDERS

Eighty-five year old Milo-native Ward Shaw played trumpet in Perley Reynolds' band from 1936 through 1938. Not just any trumpet, either. Ward played first trumpet. Here are a few of his recollections of the places he and the Commanders played:

"We played a lot at Auto Rest Park (in Carmel). We played under a big tent, where WLBZ broadcast live shows on Saturday night. Then," continues Ward, "there was the Prairie, in Brownville. It was a popular weekend dance spot located on a flat field resembling a prairie, near a former airstrip, on the Millinocket road. It had a nice fireplace, and was operated by Paul Arbo, who'd had 'BROWNVILLE' painted in large letters on the roof for approaching aircraft." But what Ward remembers best is the line of traffic: "On Saturday night there would be a stream of cars lining the road back to Brownville Junction, several miles distant." Another spot was the Gypsy, in Bucksport. About all Ward recollects of it was that "It was out of town."

Photo, BANGOR AUTO SHOW PROGRAM, March 1935 (a year before Ward joined the group). Perley Reynolds and his aggregation operated out of Bangor, billing themselves as "Maine's Leading Musical Organization." Perley himself played drums.

Island Park, Cobbosee, Me.

Postcard view, circa 1915. Billed as "Maine's Coolest, Largest, Most Beautiful Summer Dance Pavilion," Island Park played host to dancers by the thousands in its close to six decades of operation. It was, sad to say, demolished in 1971.

Al Corey and his big band at Island Park in 1948. That's Al - and his sax - standing up. Photo courtesy of Al Corey, Waterville.

Dance Halls

ISLAND PARK
WINTHROP

Some Maine dance halls are more easily recalled than others. The one that seems to be recalled the most easily of all is Island Park. Constructed in 1903 by the Winthrop & Gardiner Electric Railway Line to increase its ridership - by giving folks a fun place to go - Island Park was indeed an island park, located on an island in Lake Cobbosseecontee just off the Augusta-Lewiston Highway (present-day Routes 100 and 202).

"It was the bands and the people: the dancers." That's what made Island Park so special, back in the 1940s, for 77-year old Winthrop-native Roland Lavallee. "It was very, very nice," he adds. "I couldn't wait for Saturday night."

Patricia (Buotte) Jortberg, who'd often make her way to Island Park as a teenager from Augusta in the early 1950s, recalls the park's dance hall as "glamorous" and "exciting." She was especially in awe of the large rotating silver ball that hung over the middle of the dance floor, casting, as she puts it so majestically, "dew drops of light throughout the dance hall."

Al Corey, a Waterville native all the way, goes a step further: "It seemed to be the best dance hall in central Maine. It had a wonderful dance floor. People from all around came to Island Park." Al should know. For a dozen years, from 1948 to 1959, Al Corey and his Orchestra were Island Park's featured big band. "I thought it was a very romantic place. You drove over a small wooden bridge in your auto. You could rent a boat or enjoy the island. And the music carried all over the island." Summed up Al in a November 22, 2000 interview: "When you played Island Park you had it made. Musicians always wanted to play there."

Continued from page 34
to 5,000 square feet - dance floor on which to listen to the strains of Lennie Lizotte and his Silver Slipper Club Orchestra.

In the mid-coast area dancers were kept busy at the Ox-Horn Pavilion, in Wiscasset; Smith's Pavilion, in West Point; the Puddledock Pavilion, in Albion; LeClair's Pavilion, in Gurnet (Harpswell); Sylvester's New Dance Time, in Durham (which often featured Joe Nevil and his Alabama Aces, "The Outstanding Colored Band of the East"); Lakehurst, in Damariscotta (which advertised a recently enlarged floor with no increase in price and also assured its customers that there would be "No Parking Worries Here"); and Oakland Park, in Rockport, where on a warm July 4th evening in 1946 you could enjoy Gordon Howe, his 13-piece orchestra, and his two vocalists. Not to be outdone, the Lewiston-Auburn area provided the likes of the Spinning Wheel Dance Pavilion, four miles from Lewiston near Crowley's Junction; Pikes New Barn, in Livermore Falls; Crescent Lake Pavilion, in Webbs Mills; the White Horse Inn (with Narragansett Ale and Ruppert's Beer on draught), on Route 28 near Poland Spring; Torrey Hill, in North Turner; Elliott's Pavilion, in Dixfield; Smithy's, in Welchville (which featured George Goodie's 14-piece assemblage); the New Moon-Glo ("It's where you'll find the crowd."), in Wayne; and, swinging toward Augusta and Waterville, ever-popular Island Park, in Winthrop; the Brick Barn, in Sidney; the Lakeview Pavilion, in South China; and the Homestead, in Litchfield (which touted itself as "Maine's newest, most unique hall," with space to accommodate more than 1000 people).

Dance spots in and around Portland included the Highland Grove Pavilion, in South Standish; Steep Falls' Wildwood (where you could twirl your partner beneath a giant crystal ball); the Jack O' Lantern, in South Portland; Majestic Hall, in downtown Portland, plus, naturally, both the Pier and the Palace Ballroom, in Old Orchard.

The dancing crowds slimmed down during World War II. For starters, with so many men and women in the service, there were far less dancers to dance. Then there were, at times, shortages of the bands themselves. By 1944 the Crystal Ballroom, in Dover-Foxcroft, was running "Wanted - Dance Band To Play Saturday Nites" ads in *The Bangor Daily News*. Gas, too, was a major problem. To counter fuel shortages many of the halls stepped up their

"In the summer - on Saturday nights - we'd go to a dance hall in South China on China Lake. Lakeview. This was in the late forties, when I was still in Richmond High School. It was a summer (only) dance hall. It was right on the lake. It'd be nice and cool. They'd have all the windows open. It seemed like 100 miles from Richmond, probably because I was so anxious to get there. In the summer we'd go every Saturday night. It was a highlight. Why? Boys! And I've always loved to dance. Especially the jitterbug. Slow dances were ok, too, depending on who you were dancing with."

Ginny (Anderson) Ferris, 69, Bath
June 8, 2000

Dance Halls

bus transportation from key central city points. When the Spinning Wheel, located on Old Lisbon Road south of Lewiston, opened up for the season in July of 1944, for example, it ran shuttle busses from Peck's Department Store in downtown Lewiston every hour on the hour from 8:00 P.M. on. Auto Rest and others encouraged carpooling. Plus, pointed out Auto Rest management, holders of B ration cards who managed to save gas from their business needs were allowed to use the remaining fuel "for pleasure trips or for any other purpose they desire." All to the good. Getting out was a boost to morale. As the Turn Inn, in Hermon, made note of in its ads: "All Work and No Play Makes Jack a Dull Boy."

At the conclusion of the war in 1945 most of the world celebrated. Maine newspapers of the day contained many a "Victory Dance" announcement. The New Moon-Glo Pavilion in Wayne held a Victory Week Dance. There was a Victory Dance at the LeMontagnard Social Club in Lewiston; a Victory Show at the C-Bar-C Ranch on Route 302 in North Windham; a Victory Dance at Maccabees Hall in Bangor; a Benefit and Victory Dance at B.I.W.'s Recreation Hall in Bath; and, to top things off, a Gala Victory Dance at Wits End Dance Hall, located in - where else? - Wits End (which is, itself, located in Head Tide).

The forties ended as they had begun: with dance hall music in the air. Not just night air, but early morning air as well.

Continued on page 43

"I started in 1939 and I worked with him (Joe Avery, a popular bandleader of the day) on and off for years. I played piano. We didn't make much money, I'll tell you. We averaged $4.00 (apiece) a night.

We usually played Haye's (ed. note: "Haye's" was Haye's Open Air Casino, a dance hall of note on Knickerbocker Pond in Boothbay) every Wednesday and Saturday (during the summer). It was an excellent place. And very popular. Sometimes we'd have 500 people. It had an excellent dance floor: well-groomed and waxed. It had a snack bar. And a raised platform (for the band) so we wouldn't be run over by avid dancers.

We had eight pieces: two trumpets, three saxes, drums, stand-up bass, and piano. We were mostly from Bath and the Bath area. We were welders and mailmen and the like in real life. I was luggin' mail in the day and playing piano at night.

We had some experiences. I remember one time, around 1948, we were playing, in Camden I believe it was, and Joe was playing (drums) in the back and we heard this loud crash. We looked back and there was nothing there. We were on a raised platform and there must have been vibration and he'd (Joe) fallen off the platform, drums and all. We kept on playing. We didn't know what else to do."

Bob Rice, 75, piano player for the former Joe Avery Orchestra, June 12, 2000

AROUND THE STATE

Over the years there have probably been close to two hundred dance halls in operation in Maine. Here's a small sampling.

COY'S LANDING
SEBEC LAKE, DOVER-FOXCROFT

Postcard view, circa 1930. Courtesy of Dot Blanchard, Newcastle. Coy's Pavilion was built at Greeley's Landing on Sebec Lake by Harry Coy in 1922. It featured a hardwood floor and electric lights powered by a generator. There was a store in front. It was run by Mrs. Coy. In 1949 the pavilion was converted to a roller skating rink. It is still, today, operated as a skating rink during the summer.

Dance Halls

THE DANCEMORE
WEST BALDWIN

Postcard view, circa 1940. Built in the 1930s, the Dancemore was unique in that it had an orchestra platform that hung from the ceiling over the middle of the dance floor. The hall's slogan was "Where You Dance Under The Music." The building still stands - minus its hanging orchestra platform - on Route 113. It serves as a bingo/senior citizens' center.

1587   THE "DANCEMORE", WEST BALDWIN, MAINE

OAKLAND PARK
ROCKPORT

Photo, circa 1936. Courtesy of Ward Shaw, Brewer. As early as 1905, Oakland Park was advertised as the "Finest Spot On the Maine Coast." Later, in the 1920s, that was expanded to "Famous Picnic Resort and Pleasure Paradise," featuring parking for 1,200 cars and "Maine's Most Marvelous Moonlit Ball Room." Oakland Park continued to function, albeit on an ever-decreasing scale, into the 1950s. It closed in 1955 and is today operated as a summer-only motel/hotel/cottage complex.

BIRCH POINT PAVILION
ISLAND FALLS

'Twas there a soul in Island Falls who - at one time or another - didn't take at least one twirl around the dance floor at the Birch Point Pavilion? It's doubtful. Built in 1922 by W.P. Edwards, the Birch Point was 70 feet long and 45 feet wide. As noted by W.P.'s son, Joseph W. Edwards, "It would hold 200 people pretty good." And, as further noted by Joseph, "What a great time people had." Damaged by heavy snow in the mid-1930s, the Birch Point was rebuilt and served another two and a half decades, to 1958, when it was dismantled after again being damaged by heavy snows. As Island Falls' historian Walter O'Roak puts it: "It (the dance hall) had served its era well."

Postcard view, circa 1930. Courtesy of Peter D. Bachelder, Ellsworth. Bands that played Birch Point included Bertram Robertson and his band, from Sherman Station; Rodney Palmer and his band, from Island Falls; and the Venetian Melody Boys and Fogg's Famous Dance Band, both from Massachusetts. Walter O'Roak recounts that one of the Venetian Melody Boys fell in love with and married a local Island Falls girl. And that he and she lived - in Island Falls, of course - happily ever after.

Postcard view, circa 1930. Courtesy of Joseph W. Edwards, Island Falls. The Pavilion stood on posts and, sometimes, if the crowd got to be too many, laughs Joseph, "We would ask the band not to play any fast number."

Dance Halls

Continued from page 39

End-of-summer-season midnight dances were still aplenty. The Rhythm Rascals brought in Labor Day morn at the Twilight Pavilion's midnight-to-4:00 A.M. extravaganza in Hermon. Shoreacres, on Route 24 in Bowdoinham, advertised door prizes and "Acres of Parking Space" for its midnight special, while the New Moon-Glo, in Wayne, touted "A Better Time For Less Money" at its Monster Midnite-Dawn Dance. Other Labor Day-morning lively spots included the Villa Vaughn (at Orono Landing on Pushaw Lake); the Pier (in Belfast); the Hanger (in Trenton); Highland Grove (in South Standish); Lakeland (in North Windham); both Old Orchard's Pier and Palace Ballroom; Conant's Barn (in Paris Hill, which billed its event the Hobo Hop); the Priscilla Casino (in Auburn); and Auto Rest Park (still in Carmel).

SOUTHPORT CASINO
SOUTHPORT

Postcard view, circa 1905. Courtesy of the Boothbay Region Historical Society, Boothbay Harbor. Although constructed around 1900, well before the period of Maine's dance hall zenith, the Southport Casino served that period well, until destroyed by fire in 1937. The Casino's owner, Saul Hayes, then went on to greater glory, building Haye's Open Air Casino in Boothbay. It was a delight to mid-coast highsteppers until it, too, was destroyed by fire, in 1951.

THE LAKESIDE
LINCOLN

Ernest Lowell, who owned the Lakeside from the early 1960s until its closing in the early 1980s, believes that dancing started there during World War II. The structure had been built in 1939 as a combination arcade, bowling alley, and pool hall and, per Ernest, was "a hot spot." Ernest, whose dad Vaughn Lowell, Sr., owned and operated the Lakeside for many years before Ernest took over, recalls that during the war years there were dances every Saturday night. With "big crowds as there was no gas to go anywhere." The Lakeside featured a revolving color light suspended above the middle of the dance floor and, again per Ernest, "With the house lights out it was pretty cozy." Plus, of course, there was always a live band. One of the best remembered of those bands was the Farmers, photographed here as they appeared in 1955. From left to right that's Floyd Geary of Lincoln, trumpet; Jerry Dyer of Howland, drums; Ray Jordan of Lincoln, sax; Lawrence Nadeau of East Millinocket, sax/violin; and Beatrice LeVasseur of Howland, piano. Photo courtesy of Ernest Lowell.

The Lakeside, converted to an art studio/retail shop complex, was demolished by fire on January 17, 2002.

Dance Halls

THE GRAY ROAD INN
WEST CUMBERLAND

The Gray Road Inn (full name: Gray Road Inn and Dance Pavilion) opened on the Portland-Lewiston road in West Cumberland in June 1924. Fred Spinney was proprietor. And Fred liked catchy phrases in his ads. Among his favorites were "The Ballroom Beautiful," "Dance Lover's Paradise," and "Dancing 'Neath The Pines."
A person who would undoubtedly agree with all of the above is 74-year old Blanche Hutchins. Blanche frequented the Gray Road in the mid-1940s, even met her husband-to-be there in 1948. "The (Gray Road's) floor was large, even, real nice, with lots of young people and crowds most every night," fondly recalls Blanche, adding "It was one fun place." Sad to say, though, it's a fun place that no longer exists. Per Blanche, the Gray Road has long since been demolished.

Circa 1940 postcard view. Courtesy of Peter D. Bachelder, Ellsworth. Legend has it that the Gray Road served bootleg booze during Prohibition. Legend is probably right.

Circa 1956 postcard view. Courtesy of Blanche Hutchins, Kittery. I think it can safely be said that the Gray Road Inn and Dance Pavilion was fancier on the inside than it was on the outside.

1950s

As the second half of the 20th Century began there were few hints of the monumental changes that were to come to popular music before the decade was out. Dance halls and dance bands were still very much in evidence. But there was, if you looked closely enough, definite slippage. Fewer halls. Fewer play dates. The culprit was television. In 1950 there was a modicum of tv sets in operation. If a friend happened to have a set, he/she almost instantly became your *best* friend. By 1955 the number of sets had jumped: not many households were without easy access to "the box." Dancing often became secondary to Amos 'n Andy, George Gobel, Beat the Clock, or the Jackie Gleason Show. It was easier - and cheaper - to stay home than to "get all dressed up" and go out hoofing.

Still, though, a lot of the old standbys, plus new entries here and there, guaranteed a good time. In no particular order these good-time places included Lakehurst, in Damariscotta (which sometimes featured the popular Lloyd Rafnell and his Orchestra and sometimes featured Gerry Cram and his Orchestra); Howard's Hall, in Five Islands; Gurnet Pavilion, in Brunswick (which advertised ample parking and a "Pleasant Atmosphere"); Small Point Casino, in Phippsburg; Hayes Open-Air Casino, in Boothbay, (where you were apt to enjoy Joe Avery and his Orchestra); the Ox-Horn, on Route 1 in Wiscasset; Shoreacres, on Merrymeeting Bay in Bowdoinham (where Win Snell's Orchestra, as with so many bands of the period, played both "Modern and Square Dances"); the Riverside, in Portland (where admission was 42¢ plus tax); Crescent Lake Pavilion, in Webbs Mills; Blackstone's Pavilion, in North Yarmouth; Villa Vaughn, on Pushaw Lake; the Clary Lake Casino, in Jefferson; Danceland, in Strickland; the Lakeview Pavilion, in South China; the Whip-Poor-Will (which advertised itself as "Central Maine's Newest Dance Pavilion" and promised "Always a Crowd"), on Tacoma Lake in Litchfield; Lakeland, in North Windham (with Ozzie Miller and his Lakelanders playing all your favorites); Highland Grove, in South Standish; and Hartford's Pavilion, in Cornish (with music by the Katahdin Mountaineers); Then, of course, there was always Old Orchard Beach's danceland duo: the Palace Ballroom and the Pier. The Pier, especially, booked name bands. Among those that played the Pier in the

Dance Halls

years 1950 to 1955 were Carmen Cavallaro, Tommy and Jimmy Dorsey, Art Mooney, Vaughn Monroe, Guy Lombardo, Lionel Hampton, and the one and only Louis Armstrong. Rounding things out there was also the Hill Top Barn, in Hartford; the New Moon-Glo Pavilion, in Wayne (where Lennie Lizotte could well be holding court); Art's Barn, between Livermore Falls and Farmington on Route 133; the Shady Nook, in West Newfield; the Blue Bird Dance Pavilion, on Route 26 between South Paris and Bryant Pond; Joe Libby's, on Route 106 in Strickland (with admission 60¢ before 9:00; 75¢ thereafter); Priscilla's Casino, in Auburn; the Jackie Nichols Lodge, in Richmond; the Starlight Dance Pavilion, in Lagrange; (often featuring Bob Jones and his Bobcats,"The Biggest Little Band in Maine"); the Hanger, in Trenton; Ellsworth's Hancock House (where you might end up dancing to "Cool Refreshing Hawaiian Music" as played by the Tropical Serenaders); the Gypsy, in Bucksport, Island Park, on the Augusta-Winthrop road (with Bob Percival's Band and "Sensational Vocalist" Janet Lund); Auto Rest Park, in Carmel; Gowan's Pavilion, in North Bradford; the Log Lodge, in Lucerne-in-Maine; the Bar-L Ranch, in Newport; the York Beach Casino, in York Beach; Dover-Foxcroft's Crystal Ballroom; Goodwin's, also in Dover-Foxcroft; the Farm, in Mattawamkeag (where you could hear "Alf" Afholderbach and his Orchestra); Twilight Pavilion, in Hermon; the Bandbox Pavilion, in Norway; the Hill Top Barn, in Canton; and the Breezemere Pavilion, which brightened Route 137 in Lincolnville Beach and which promised Good Music and Old and New Dances, and all for 50¢, tax included.

Ad, *Portland Press Herald*, July 10, 1965. Ansel G. Morton (1892-1975) owned and operated Morton's Pavilion for over 50 years. And, come Saturday night, he usually played a mean fiddle in the band, too. His pavilion yet operates today as Remember When.

DANCING
EVERY SAT. NITE
Where It's Fun
MORTON'S PAVILION
— NAPLES —
Featuring
"JOEY"
And The Country Playboys

47

Rock 'n Roll Arrives On The Scene

In 1955 there occurred an event of mammoth proportions in the world of music. One day America was listening to the Hilltoppers, Joni James, Eddie Fisher, and the Dorseys. And the next day - or so it seemed - America was listening to Fats Domino, the El Dorados, the Moonglows, Bo Diddley, and Bill Haley and the Comets. Young America, anyway.

How did the arrival of rock 'n roll effect Maine's dance halls and dancers? Seemingly not much. Not at the outset, anyway. It was, after all, the teenagers who were "hip" into Fats et al. More settled folk just kept on doing what they had been doing. By the late 1950s, though, many dance halls were singing the blues. A combination of aging audience, more and better tv, and the lure of the drive-in theatre was taking its toll.

A list of those Maine halls still in operation in 1958-1959 would include the old reliable Auto Rest Park, in Carmel; the Hanger, in Trenton; the New Moon Pavilion (which billed itself as "Maine's Largest Ballroom"), on Route 16 in Alton; the Bar-L, in Newport; the Farm, in Mattawamkeag; Goodwin's, in Dover-Foxcroft; Twilight Pavilion, on Hermon Pond; Songo Pond Pavilion, (located between Bethel and Waterford and which noted "The Crowd Goes Where The Fun Is"); old friend Island Park, on the Augusta-Winthrop Highway; the Riverview Casino at Sebasco Estates; the Gypsy, in Bucksport; Lakehurst (still going strong featuring Lloyd Rafnell and his Orchestra), in Damariscotta; Riverside, in Portland; Highland Grove, in South Standish; Lakeland, in North Windham; the Blue Goose, in Northport; the Umbrella, located on Sanborn Pond east of Belfast and which touted itself as "a Unique Dance Pavilion;" and, last but never least, Old Orchard Beach's wonderful pair, the Pier and the Palace Ballroom.

What was most noticeable was the almost complete absence, by the late 1950s, of that old tradition, the day-before-Labor Day midnight-to-dawn "frolic." I could find but two 1959 instances: at the Pier, and at Morton's Pavilion, in Naples, (where Little Joey and the Country Playboys kept things going 'til dawn's early light). By contrast, there were at least six drive-in theatres throughout the state that featured what several of them cleverly called a "Giant Dusk To Yawn Show." One drive-in, the Bowdoin, in Brunswick, even served free coffee at dawn.

Dance Halls

THE 1960s

The 1960s saw the continued decline of dance halls and dance bands. Neither Motown nor "The British Invasion" helped. The Beatles, the Rolling Stones, and the Dave Clark Five did not clamor to play the Bar-L or Morton's Pavilion. Old favorites such as Lakehurst (Damariscotta), Auto Rest Park (Carmel), and the Pier and the Palace (Old Orchard) struggled on. The Palace mixed live bands with record hops, while the Pier was more apt to continue on with big name performers. Other dance hall strongholds included the New Cedars (Durham); Jollytime (in Otisfield, where for 60¢ admission you could enjoy "Music by the Music Men"); Morton's Pavilion (Naples); Blackstone Hall (on Route 9 on the North Yarmouth-Pownal line); and Lakeland (in North Windham, where you and yours could dance to your heart's content to the Katahdin Mountaineers).

The mid-sixties saw the continuance of Morton's Pavilion, in Naples; Melody Lane, in St. Albans; and the Umbrella Dance Hall (featuring Fidlin' Harold's Bear Trappers every Saturday night), between Belfast and Brooks on Route 137. Then there was the High Spot, in Bradley; Happy Acres, on Route 16 in Alton; and the Rosedall Music Barn (which featured Joe Avery's Orchestra, and advertised "Adults Only"), in West Bath.

As the 1960s waned and 1970 arrived there were still some dance halls open and operating. These included the Top Hat Pavilion, in Hanover; the Long Beach Pavilion ("In The Pines"), on Route 126 in Sabattus; Crowley's Junction, in South Lewiston; Lakeland, in North Windham; the venerable Palace Ballroom, in Old Orchard; the Bar-L (with Don Tardy and the Lincoln Troubadours), in Newport; the Puddledock, in Albion; the Rainbow Dance Hall ("Featuring Old-Time Dance Music"), in Readfield Depot; the Ox Bow, on Route 46 in Bucksport; and the Red Barn (which prohibited shorts, slacks, culottes, pant dresses and "male stags"), in the thick of things in Monroe.

For the most part, though, if you wanted to do some dancing you were apt to have to settle for a veterans' or fraternal club. Or a restaurant/lounge. It was ok. But it really wasn't the same as the sounds of Gordon Howe or Al Corey or Perley Reynolds wafting across the dance floor at Lakehurst, Island Park, Auto Rest Park, or the Pier.

WESTLEIGH'S
AUCTION BARN
DANCE HALL

CARRYING ON THE DANCE HALL TRADITION

While Maine dance halls do not abound as they once did, there are still quite a few in operation in one form or another. Some are full-time dance halls, open two or three nights a week. Some open up once a month. Others open "on demand," when a band or organization rents the hall and hopefully makes a go of it by charging admission. Many old-time dance halls now also bill themselves as "function halls," rentable for special occasions such as weddings, anniversaries, family reunions, etc. They may, as well, double as an auction hall. And most operate pretty much the same all year around: winter activity - or inactivity - is not very different than summer.

Shown here are photos, all taken in spring/summer, 2001, of some of the dance halls yet in operation across the state. Others in operation, but not pictured here, include: Crystal Falls, Chelsea; Deer Isle-Stonington

Dance Halls

Center, Stonington; Echo Hill Dance Hall, St. George; Lakehurst, Damariscotta; Melody Ballroom/Ranch (called Melody Ranch on Fridays, when there's country & western bands; Melody Ballroom on Sundays, when there's big bands: pretty clever), Fairfield Center; the Red Barn, Monroe; Remember When, Naples; The Roost, Buxton; Wesley Dance Hall, Wesley; The Nickolodeon, Mechanic Falls; and Wildwood, Steep Falls.

There are undoubtedly, I hope, others as well. So put on your dancing shoes. And if you've thrown them away? Well, just imagine how snappy you'd look in a new pair!

Photos, left to right:
Blue Goose (Northport); sign, Westleigh's Auction Barn & Dance Hall (Arundel); Crossroads (Standish); 10-4 Dance Hall (Montville); sign, Lobster Ranch (Harrington); sign, Blue Haven (Wiscasset); sign, Harmony Hall (North Yarmouth)

"I recall when I was about nine or ten, in 1945 or 1946, my parents and I were driving along the road on our way to Biddeford and I saw this big thing by the side of the road. I said 'What's that?' And my mother said 'That's a drive-in movie theatre. You can sit in your car and watch movies.' I was so thrilled with that. That you could sit in your car and watch a movie."

Jeanette (Burke) Dufour
Yarmouth
March 15, 2001

Drive-Ins

Circa 1935 drive-in
advertising art

SEE THE STARS UNDER THE STARS: MAINE AND THE DRIVE-IN THEATRE

The Birth of the Drive-In

Richard M. Hollingshead, Jr. (1900-1975) was a man with a mission. The time was the early 1930s, the Great Depression was weighing heavy, and Hollingshead was less than fully enthralled with his job. But he had an idea that excited him. Marry those two great American passions, the automobile and the movies, he reasoned, and people would come by the drove. Depression or no Depression.

After a period of experimentation with a projector and a screen in the front yard of his house in Riverton, New Jersey, Hollingshead and his cousin, Willis W. Smith, formed Park-In Theatres, Inc.. They then proceeded to construct the world's first drive-in, which they named the Automobile Movie Theatre, on a ten-acre site on Crescent Boulevard (now Admiral Wilson Boulevard) in Camden, New Jersey. The Grand Opening was June 6, 1933, and an estimated six-hundred paying customers turned out for the history-making event. The price was 25¢ a car plus 25¢ a person, with a maximum of $1.00. The feature was a three-year old ditty entitled "WIFE BEWARE," starring Adolphe Menjou.

The fact that Hollingshead's first feature was a dated one foretold what was to be one of the drive-in's biggest problems: film distributors, partial to the established "hardtop" (as traditional indoor theatres were called in the trade) operators, were generally reluctant to offer first-rate fare for drive-in viewing. And when they did they often charged exorbitant fees. Hollingshead didn't do the growth of the drive-in any favors, either: he obtained a

Continued on page 56

53

WHEN DRIVE-INS WERE BUSTING OUT ALL OVER

In the five-year period between 1949 and 1954 drive-in theatres were growing by leaps and bounds all across America. Needless to say, Maine was there doing her share. Shown here are a half-dozen Maine "gala opening" ads, with, left to right, each theatre's opening date: Starlite Drive-In (Madison), June 30, 1949; Waterville Drive-In (Winslow), July 26, 1949; E.M. Loew's Bangor-Brewer Drive-In (Brewer), July 4, 1950; Lewiston Drive-In (Lewiston), July 1, 1949;

Gala OPENING TONIGHT

TUES., JULY 26 — GATES OPEN 7 P. M.

* No Charge For Cars

* **NO BABY SITTER PROBLEM!**
You can now take the children with you!
Have them under your own watchful eyes!

* **NO MORE PARKING WORRIES!**
You can now enjoy the show in the comfort of your own car.

* **INDIVIDUAL SPEAKER FOR EACH CAR!**
You adjust the volume to suit your own taste.

GRAND OPENING PROGRAM

Romance ON THE High Seas — JACK CARSON JANIS PAIGE with DeFORE — PLUS — PHOTO-FINISH THRILLS! Racing Luck

Admission Adults 50¢ inc. tax Children Under 12 Free

WATERVILLE Drive-In THEATRE AUGUSTA RD. WINSLOW

Two Technicolor Cartoons On Every Program

CONTINUOUS DUSK TILL MIDNITE

GRAND OPENING
FRIDAY NITE, JULY 1
STARLITE
DRIVE-IN THEATRE
LAKEWOOD ROAD, MADISON
2 Shows Every Night
Open at 7:30—Show Starts at 9
ADM. 50¢ tax inc.

OPENS TOMORROW at 7:30 P.M.

E.M. LOEW'S BANGOR-BREWER **DRIVE-IN** Theatre ON ROUTE 1 BREWER NEW ENGLAND'S *LARGEST and FINEST* DRIVE-IN Theatre

CONTINUOUS RAIN OR CLEAR

ADMISSION 50¢ CARS FREE

GRAND OPENING PROGRAM!
2-MIGHTY TECHNICOLOR TRIUMPHS
FIRST TIME TOGETHER!
MARIA MONTEZ **ALI BABA AND THE 40 THIEVES** TURHAN BEY
$10,000,000 TECHNICOLOR SHOW
PHANTOM OF THE OPERA CAST OF THOUSANDS
SIT IN YOUR CAR and ENJOY the MOVIES
WORLD'S LARGEST SCREEN
INDIVIDUAL SPEAKER For every car.

BRING THE FAMILY
COME DRESSED AS YOU PLEASE
SMOKE-EAT-RELAX IN THE COMFORT
OF YOUR CAR-IN CAR SPEAKERS
CHILDREN UNDER 12 - FREE

STARTS FRIDAY "WHITE HEAT" "KISS IN THE DARK"

Drive-Ins

SPECTACULAR DISPLAY OF **FIREWORKS** OPENING NITE

Gala **OPENING** TONIGHT

JULY 1st
Gate Opens 7 P.M.

No Charge For Cars

ENJOY THE MOVIES IN YOUR CAR
Relax! Smoke and dress as you please in the privacy of your own car.

NO MORE BABY SITTER PROBLEM
Bring the children with you. Two cartoons on every program.
Admission free for children under 12.

INDIVIDUAL SPEAKERS FOR EVERY CAR
Yes! You regulate the sound to your own individual taste.

GRAND OPENING PROGRAM

SATURDAY EVENING POST story!

CORONER CREEK
Starring RANDOLPH SCOTT MARGUERITE CHAPMAN
CINECOLOR

BUD **ABBOTT** — LOU **COSTELLO**
Their BIGGEST, BALMIEST HIT! Their most gay-antic roles!
Pardon My Sarong
with VIRGINIA BRUCE

LEWISTON *Drive-In* **THEATRE** on *SABATTUS RD.*

Price 50¢ Incl. Tax Children Under 12 FREE

Two Technicolor Cartoons On Every Program xxxx Shows Nightly Rain or Clear

CONTINUOUS DUSK TILL MIDNITE

★ **BRUNSWICK** **DRIVE-IN** Theatre

SHOWS NIGHTLY RAIN or MOON
ADM. 50¢

GALA OPENING TONIGHT
Portland Road, Brunswick

FRIDAY-SATURDAY   MAY 26-27

"UNTAMED BREED"
plus
"GIVE MY REGARDS TO BROADWAY"
TWO TECHNICOLOR FEATURES
TWO COLOR CARTOONS

Gates Open 7.00 p. m.   Phone 1182-W1K

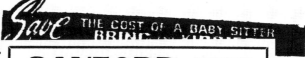

Save THE COST OF A BABY SITTER
BRING THE KIDDIES

SANFORD DRIVE-IN THEATRE
LOWER MAIN ST.   ROUTE 109   SANFORD

GALA OPENING
SUN., MAY 7

SUNDAY and MONDAY, MAY 7 and 8

EDMOND O'BRIEN ROBERT STACK in **"FIGHTER SQUADRON"** IN TECHNICOLOR

ADDED FEATURE   "VARIETY TIME" – PLUS CARTOON

LATEST IN-CAR SPEAKERS
BOTTLE WARMING SERVICE FOR BABIES

CHILDREN UNDER 12 **ADMITTED FREE**

MODERN REFRESHMENT BAR

SHOW STARTS AT DUSK

(RAIN OR SHINE)

Brunswick Drive-In (Brunswick), May 26, 1950; and Sanford Drive-In (Sanford), May 7, 1950.

Continued from page 53

patent on his invention, charging potential operators an upfront fee plus a percentage of revenue. The result was that drive-ins were few and very far between, with an estimated less than fifty in operation in the entire country by the time World War II - and gas rationing - rolled around.

In the late forties and early fifties, however, the drive-in's fortunes changed considerably. First came the burgeoning growth of auto-related business: in the wake of post-war prosperity everyone, it seemed, had a car and everyone, it seemed, wanted to spend as much time as possible in it. Secondly, in 1949 the U.S. Supreme Court ruled that the drive-in theatre was not a patentable idea. Open air theatres could now be built by anybody who wanted to build one. And a lot of people decided they wanted to. Growth was explosive.

From a peak of close to five thousand units in operation in 1958, the drive-in industry has shrunk. Considerably. Television, video rentals, multi-plex cinemas, "passion pit" reputation... all have taken their toll. Escalating real estate values on the urban fringe - prime turf for drive-ins - have also hurt considerably. Plus there's the very nature of the drive-in: it's seasonal in much of the country; dependent upon good weather in all of it.

Still, on a warm summer night, there's nothing quite like rounding up the family or your best beau and taking in a double feature down at the drive-in.

Maine Joins In

Maine was - and is - part of the drive-in scenario. The Saco Drive-In was one of the very earliest drive-ins anywhere. Opened in July of 1939, it would, however, be Maine's sole "ozoner" - the term often used for drive-ins - for a full eight years. By then, after World War II, a pent-up desire to have kids and have fun, too, kicked in. The result: beginning with the now-long-forgotten Pines in Woolwich in 1947, Maine's entrepreneurs took to opening a raft of theatres where mom and dad and the kiddies could "watch the stars under the stars." By 1949 there were 14 drive-ins in Maine. By 1953; 33. By 1955; 38.

Following is the "biography" of each of those pioneers, plus others that joined after 1955. The total comes to 47, not bad for a state with a low population and an abundance of "Closed For The Season" months. Enjoy the stories and memories.

P.S. It is well worthy of note that the Saco Drive-In is the third-oldest still-in-operation drive-in theatre in the world. Only Shankweiler's Drive-In (located in Orefield, Pennsylvania; in operation since 1934) and the Lynn Drive-In (located in Strasburg, Ohio; in operation since 1937) have seen more summers than Saco.

Circa 1930 Whiz shock absorber fluid can.

WHIZ

Had the firm that manufactured and marketed shock absorber fluid and other WHIZ auto care products been more of a challenge to its general manager, the drive-in theatre might never have come to happen. That's because the firm was the R.M. Hollingshead Corp., located in Camden, New Jersey, and founded by R.M., Jr.'s father, R.M. Hollingshead, Sr.. R.M., Jr. was the company's general manager, a position he liked but did not love. The result was his decision to pursue his dream of the drive-in. We are the richer for it.

NEW PALACE

Opening Today, August 4 of Bangor's Only Open-Air Theatre

TWO MASTERLY FEATURES THAT WILL FURNISH THE THRILLS

QUO VADIS Three Acts. The Story of the Christian Martyrs. A Stupendous Production.

BLANCHE WALSH in RESURRECTION

Four Parts. Tolstoy's Immortal Drama.

Evenings Only, Weather Permitting. First Show 7.15 P. M Admission 5c

Ad, *The Bangor Daily News*, August 4, 1913. Before there was Saco there was the New Palace.

SACO DRIVE-IN
SACO

Maine's outdoor movie theatre heritage actually goes back to – are you ready for this? – 1913. That's the year someone mistook Bangor for Miami Beach and opened the New Palace Theatre in the Lumber City's downtown. You see, the New Palace was an open-air affair. While it had walls, it was, as its advertisements trumpeted, "The Theatre Without A Roof." It was, in its own way, a rather nifty idea. But one that was hardly practical for Bangor. The theatre's opening day of August 4th was, in fact, postponed because of rain. By early September it was obvious the New Palace (later the Park) was far from a smash success. The theatre was closed "for renovations" and, complete with a roof, opened later in 1913.

It would be 26 years before the next open-air movie theatre arrived in Maine. It was a rather historic arrival, though: the Saco Auto Theatre/Motor In is thought to have been the fifth drive-in in New England – proceeded only by the Weymouth Drive-In Theatre (1936); the Lynn Open Air Theater (1937); the Providence Drive-In (1937); the Shrewsbury Drive-In (1938); and the Merrimack Auto Theatre (Methuen, 1938) – and among the first 20 in the entire country.

Saco's drive-in opened on July 15, 1939 with

Drive-Ins

Ad, *Biddeford Daily Journal*, July 15, 1939.
The drive-in had arrived in Maine!

GRAND — OPENING — TONIGHT

Maine's First

OPEN—AIR Automobile THEATRE

ON ROUTE 1 BETWEEN SACO AND PORTLAND
——NEAR ANGELLMERE——

July 15-16-17-18
Jimmy (Schnozzle) Durante
with June Clyde in
"FORBIDDEN MUSIC"
Latest News - Disney Cartoon
and Novelty

Avoid Parking Troubles
Sit in your own car and
Enjoy the Talkies
Admission
Per Person **35c**
Children under 12
and Cars Free

Continuous Every Night from Dusk 'Till Midnight
Motor in Anytime After 7

Jimmy Durante and June Clyde starring in a comedy named FORBIDDEN MUSIC. Plus there was "Latest News," a Disney cartoon, and a second novelty film. For its first several showings the theatre's ads included no name. The theatre was simply billed as "Maine's First Open-Air Automobile Theatre." The drive-in's opening came at an opportune time: the showing of movies on Sunday in Maine was legalized that very same month of July 1939. Within a week the theatre had a name. It was the Saco Open Air Auto Theatre. But the name

"Motor In" was often used as well. J. Frank Moore, a veteran theatre operator in Portland and a resident of Biddeford, was manager. In 1941 the theatre saw a change in ownership. The new proprietor was Harold Armistead, a long-time Boston-area theatre man. In the June 28, 1941 issue of the *Biddeford Daily Journal* Mr. Armistead is quoted as saying that "Only clean, wholesome pictures which the whole family may enjoy" would be shown. The article also noted that the theatre had been refitted with "the latest sound equipment." It all paid

59

Clockwise from upper left: ad, *Portland Sunday Telegram*, Oct. 1, 1939; ad, *Portland Sunday Telegram*, Oct. 15, 1939; ad, *Portland Sunday Telegram*, Oct. 7, 1939. Early on drive-ins would sometimes turn to films not likely to be shown at the local State, Strand, or Bijou. Often it was a case of taking something sensationalistic or taking nothing at all: outdoor theatres were very much on the low end of the totem pole when it came to motion picture distribution.

Drive-Ins

off: a story in the August 16th *Daily Journal* announced that "The Motor-In Theatre has just established a new high for attendance during the past ten days."

As with so many other businesses across America, the drive-in closed "for the duration" during World War II. It opened up – now named the Saco Auto Theatre – on Decoration Day 1946. The theatre's movie that evening pretty much said it all: IT'S A PLEASURE, starring Sonja Henie and Michael O'Shea. Plus there were, of course, "Selected Short Subjects."

Almost six and a half decades later Saco's contribution to drive-in theatre legend lives on. Its name became the Saco Drive-In in April of 1952. The marvelous near-the-entranceway cascading waterfall, complete with deer and a polar bear (that said to all concerned that the theatre was built as a showplace) has seen better days. On any given nice spring/summer/fall evening, though, cars filled with families or folks on a date yet make their way along Route

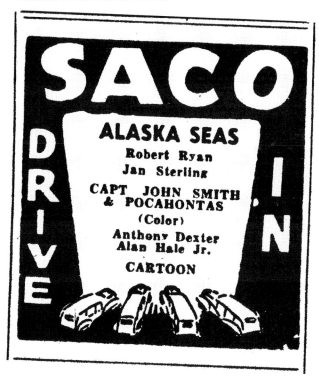

Ad, *Portland Press Herald*, May 8, 1954. This was the drive-in's newspaper advertising format in the mid-1950s.

1 to the venerable theatre. Do they care that they're a part of history? And helping to keep tradition rolling into the future? I doubt it. As long as the sky is clear, the movie good, and the popcorn hot there's not much else that really matters.

THE PINES DRIVE-IN WOOLWICH

"It was very primitive. There was no playground. Just the screen and the projection shack." That's how 82-year old Lin Temple of Bath describes the Pines, adding "I don't think there were more than a dozen cars there the night we (Lin and his wife, Barbara) were there."

The Pines was indeed primitive. But it was pioneer primitive: the Pines was the second drive-in in Maine, opening in June of 1947. It was the creation of one Bob Westfall. Bob, a Woolwich native, returned home from the service in 1945. "He liked to put on shows. And he was into cameras and photography," recalls Hayden Temple (a second cousin of Lin's), who worked at the drive-in as a kid.

Bob's grandfather, Charles Pearce, owned a tract of land off Days Ferry Road. Together the two, grandfather and grandson, built the theatre behind Charles' house. "The theatre was his dream. He (Bob) wanted to experiment," reflects Hayden.

The dream materialized on June 29, 1947. On the screen Bob and his granddad had fashioned was a film called TORTURE SHIP. There was no article in *The Bath Daily Times*. No grand opening hoopla. People in Woolwich, however,

Ad, *The Bath Daily Times*, Sept. 20, 1947. "If you missed it before" is a good example of a drive-in trying to "dress up" an old movie. ALGIERS was first released in 1938!

SATURDAY – SUNDAY
NEW STARTING TIME—7.30 TO 12 P.M.

"ALGIERS"
Charles Boyer — Hedy Lamarr
If You Missed It Before See It Now
AT
THE PINES DRIVE IN THEATRE
WOOLWICH

were well aware of Bob's presence. "There were four big speakers," laughs Hayden. "You could hear them all over town. Plus he played music - records - before and after the show. He played the same songs every show. One song I especially recall was *Bye, Bye Blackbird*. Everybody in town knew *Bye, Bye Blackbird*."

Bob's dream ended the summer of 1950. "The Brunswick Drive-In opened and stole all the business," explains Hayden Temple. "They were more modern, with individual (in car) speakers and not so many bugs."

Bob Westfall died in Bath, aged 53, on November 30, 1979. In his obituary in the *Bath-Brunswick Times Record* there was not even a mention of his pioneering efforts that summer of '47.

Drive-Ins

NAPLES DRIVE-IN
NAPLES

Russell Martin (1921-1984) was one of the more important men in Maine drive-in movie theatre history. The Gorham native sired - if you will - the rather grand total of four Vacationland ozoners. When I asked Russell's daughter, Sharon (Martin) Remick, what so intrigued her dad about outdoor movie theatres, she pondered a moment or two and then replied, "Daddy just always liked to get into things that were new. He," she went on, "liked to do different things... different from other jobs. His family owned a farm, but he didn't want to be a farmer. He wanted to be on his own; be his own boss."

Drive-in venture number one was Naples. Russell and his wife Leatrice opened for

Naples Drive-In Theatre

Route 302   Naples, Maine

Closing Attraction

SILVER SKATES

starring

KENNY BAKER; BELITA, Queen of the Ice World;
IRENE DARE; with TED FIO RITO and His Orchestra
Built around an entertaining and clean-cut story, this film
is really a dainty dish of skates and song

1t36x

Ad, *The Bridgton News*, Sept. 3, 1948. This was the theatre's last ad for its first year and whoever wrote the wording was having some fun - "a dainty dish of skates and song" - with it.

business on Friday, June 25, 1948. The first film was JACK LONDON, starring Susan Hayward and Michael O'Shea. Per Sharon, the theatre was simple. Just the basics. "They (her parents) put speakers on top of their car," Sharon relays. Still, Russell and Leatrice's Naples Drive-In was the third drive-in in the state and the first one inland, away from the coastline. According to an article in *The Bridgton News*, the drive-in was situated on but four acres and showed a movie every night of the week but Thursday. In the article Russell is quoted as saying: "The drive-in theatre seems to have been especially designed for families with babies. No more worries about getting a babysitter. Pack the baby in the old jalopy, and be off to an evening at the movies with no worries. Some folks even bring their cats and dogs."

The Naples Drive-In was not to be long on the scene. The Martins closed it after the season of 1949, moving operations to Sanford and opening the Sanford Drive-In (q.v.) in 1950. Sharon isn't really sure why the switch. She thinks it may have been because her mom and dad lived in Sanford, or that they considered Sanford a better market.

The Naples Drive-in's former location, on Route 302 about a mile southeast of downtown, is now occupied by Sydney's Restaurant and Pub.

63

Photo, most likely May, 1949. Courtesy of Priscilla Bucklin, Sanford. Priscilla rummaged through mounds of old snapshots to find this Norman Rockwell-ish shot of the theatre's signboard being painted. "He (Leonard) liked to take pictures of things," noted Priscilla.

ACTON DRIVE-IN
ACTON

Maine's shortest-lived known drive-in was the dream of Sanford natives Ralph Ross and Leonard Bucklin. Especially Leonard. "He was always interested in movies," his widow Priscilla told me in a September 2001 interview. And that interest was fanned toward the end of World War II when Leonard was stationed in the Air Force in Okinawa. His base had but a primitive outdoor theatre set-up and none of the good movies. The Navy got all of those. Leonard went to his commanding officer and got permission to try to get better films. And he did. "That's where he really got the (movie) bug," laughs Priscilla. After his service stint Leonard came home and started law school in Portland. He had the summers off, however, and he and old pal and fellow law student, Ralph, came up with the idea of a drive-in.

The Acton Drive-In was far from a showplace.

Situated on a small slice of the Acton Fairgrounds, it was, in Priscilla's words, "basic." Longtime friend and sometime projectionist Howard Littlefield, 84, goes a step further down the rating scale. He terms the theatre "bare bones." There was a tiny projection booth, two or three large speakers, and a homemade screen. Neither Priscilla nor Howard could recall whether there was a ticket booth or, in fact, how tickets were sold.

The theatre's initial showing was May 27, 1949. On the screen was GYPSY WILDCAT, starring Maria Montez and Jon Hall. Thirteen weeks later, on September 1st, it all ended. What does Priscilla recall about that summer of 1949? "I took our three young kids to the drive-in in pj's," she reminisces. "They slept in the car. And it was a Crosley." She quickly adds, "Do you know how small a Crosley is?!" (ed. note: the Crosley was a pioneer economy car. Manufactured from 1939 to 1952, it was *very* small.).

The Acton Drive-In ceased operations after the one season because business was not brisk ("Business was not rushing" is how Howard puts it.), and because Leonard (1924-2001) graduated from law school in the spring of 1950 and went immediately into law practice. On the drive-in's old site on Route 109 and 12th Street there is still the Acton Fairgrounds. You can load up your car and come on out for the fair in late August. There'll be food and fun but - by over five decades - you will have missed the last picture show.

Ad, *Sanford Tribune and Advocate*, June 11, 1949. Priscilla and Howard remember Leonard and Ralph as doing no advertising. But they did… in the weekly *Sanford Tribune and Advocate*. This ad was for week number three. There would be eleven weeks left.

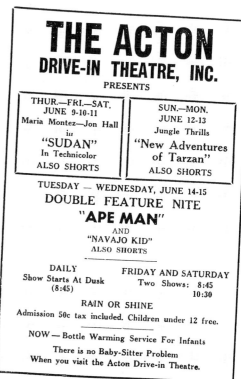

Stock certificate. Courtesy of Priscilla Bucklin, Sanford. Leonard and Ralph sold shares in their endeavor. It turned out not to be the wisest of investments.

BORDERLAND DRIVE-IN HOULTON

Houlton's contribution to outdoor movieland was the Borderland Drive-In. "It was a good idea and filled a need in the area for families," says Lewis Webber when asked why he and his partner, Harold Peabody, opened the drive-in in 1949. On May 28, 1949. Lewis will also tell you that the Borderland was the first drive-in north of Bangor and the second, after Saco, in the state. He's proud of both. Alas, though, he's wrong regarding "the second in the state." The Pines, Naples, and Acton had all opened earlier.

At first Lewis and Harold relied on a single speaker mounted on top of the screen. It didn't work. In 1952 they installed individual in-car speakers, 400 of them. Admission was 35¢ to start with, and worked its way up to all of $1.00 toward the drive-in's waning days. All along, recalls regular attendee Lynn York, there'd be a special "Buck Night" every Thursday. "Everyone who could fit in the car for one buck," emphasizes Lynn. "And it

Photo, circa 1952. That's Lewis, his daughter Nina, wife Nola, and aunt Alice in front of the refreshment stand. You can see part of the Moonglow atop the stand's roof. Foodwise, the stand was best known for its home-cut/home-cooked French fries. At one point, figures Lewis, Nola and her crew were going through a barrel of potatoes a day. Both photos courtesy of Lewis Webber, Naples, Florida.

Photo, circa 1952. Aunt Alice and Lewis' son Alan on the theatre's seesaw. "We had a fairly good-sized playground," recalls Lewis. "with three or four swings, monkey bars, and a slippery slide."

Drive-Ins

was a success," he fondly recalls. "There were lines of cars two miles down the road in both directions. They used to have a sheriff or two to direct traffic from both ways. It," per Lynn, "was wild!"

What Lynn also fondly recalls is the Borderland's concession stand. "It was all run by Lewis' - everybody called him "Ike" - wife Nola and her sisters." In addition to the goodies prepared by Nola and company, there was, again per Lynn, a pole on top of the stand. And on top of that was a light. Actually four lights, from four great big lightbulbs. "It was up in the air 50 feet or so. And," continues Lynn, "it was called the Moonglow. It gave off a really unusual lighting effect - almost like a rainbow - at intermission. It was unique," sums up Lynn, "kind of his (Ike's) signature."

Lewis Webber sold the drive-in in 1979. "I could foresee a decline (in attendance) due to tv and vcrs," he says. "Plus I was at retirement age."

In its second life, the Borderland ran until 1985. For many years thereafter the theatre's grounds were used by the local Military Street Baptist Church for Sunday morning services. Even that stopped four or five years ago. The screen and all its outbuildings now stand empty.

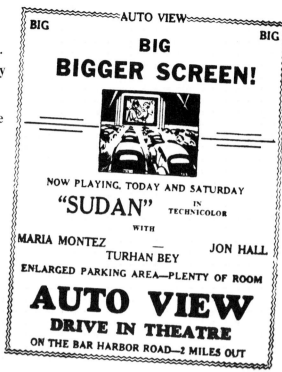

Ad, *The Bangor Daily News*, July 1, 1949. Before the Ellsworth-Trenton was the Ellsworth-Trenton it was the Auto View.

ELLSWORTH-TRENTON DRIVE-IN TRENTON

The Ellsworth-Trenton Drive-In enjoyed a checkered life. First of all, it opened not as the Ellsworth-Trenton, but as the Auto View. Grand Opening was June 4, 1949. The theatre advertised, in BIG type, that there was "A Complete Refreshment Stand For Your Enjoyment." In much smaller type there was a "thank you" to Kenneth Lord, of Patten, the winner in management's name-the-theatre contest.

As the Auto View the drive-in remained in operation a little over a year. In early August 1950 the theatre, due to-lack of support on the part of the paying public, shut down. It wasn't until two years later, on June 7, 1952, that the theatre re-opened... as the Ellsworth-Trenton. New owner Sam Nyer, now 75, recalls it well: "A year or so after I started Enfield (the Enfield Drive-In, q.v.) a man named Harriman wanted to sell me this drive-in he owned in Trenton. He wanted $5,000 for it. So I went and looked at it and I said 'The screen looks wobbly.' And he (the owner) said 'I built that screen myself and I'd bet my life it'll stay up.' Well, about three weeks after I'd bought it I get a call from the state police at 1:00 in the morning. There'd been a windstorm and the screen had blown down and was all over the highway." So much for betting ones life.

Another person who remembers is 81-year old Virginia Davis. Virginia now lives in Orono, but she used to live in Trenton. And she worked at the drive-in for 33 years! "We had a lot of good pictures," she says with pride. "We had AROUND THE WORLD IN 80 DAYS. And we played THE GREATEST SHOW ON EARTH. We ran that for several weeks." Continues Virginia: "For most of the good ones (movies) people would come at 4:00 in the afternoon and bring their supper and eat 'til the show started. We'd get enough people to fill up the parking lot, which held 250 cars."

Virginia also recalls the age-old problem of kids sneaking in. "We had a lot of people that would try to sneak in. But," chuckles Virginia, "there was a lady who ran a nearby restaurant where kids would buy soda and/or snacks, and she'd call and say 'There's three in the trunk of such and such a car.' So they'd drive up and buy two tickets and I'd say 'What about the three in the trunk?' Were they embarrassed? No, they thought they were being cute."

What most people seem to remember about the Ellsworth-Trenton Drive-In is DEEP THROAT, the X-rated flick that featured Linda Lovelace doing her thing. The theatre first showed it on June 19, 1974. It was so successful that Sam showed it over... and over... and over. It wasn't until the tail end of September that the drive-in made the switch to another feature. At the end of the season, per Maine history aficiando Dick Shaw of Bangor, someone had the words "Clothed For The Winter" put up on the drive-in's signboard.

Eventually Clothed became Closed. The end for the Ellsworth-Trenton came on September 6, 1984. "We weren't getting any attendance," sums up Virginia Davis.

Drive-Ins

POLARIS DRIVE-IN
CARIBOU

The Polaris was the creation of Mapleton native Lewis Christie. Lewis was a mail carrier and potato farmer in the years following World War II. Then the federal government decided there were too many potato farmers in Maine. Lewis was one of those told to cease production. It was not a request. "It was a must," Lewis' wife Gertrude makes very clear. What to do? Well, Lewis had been to a drive-in in Massachusetts a few years earlier. "He thought," says Gertrude, "that (building and running a drive-in) would be a nice thing to do."

The Polaris opened for business on June 10, 1949. One of the crowd when she was a youngster was Caribou native Jean Jacobs. Jean, now 52, recalls that the theatre's speakers often provided less than optimum sound and that her family oftimes had to move once or twice to find a speaker that "spoke." Jean also laughs as she recalls trips to the restroom and how strange it was seeing the big screen but hearing nothing.

Lewis Christie ran the Polaris until 1966, when he sold to Ashland-native Charlie Brooks who, in turn, sold to Larry Cyr. That was circa 1981.

Larry had also purchased the Dorseyland, changing its name to the Hilltop. Larry's plan, alas, was to focus on the Hilltop. "We only ran the Polaris one summer," he told me in a phone interview in December 2000. "There just wasn't enough business for two drive-ins. So I closed and tore down the smaller and older of the two." Today the Polaris' former site, about $1/2$ mile southeast of Russell's Motel on old Route 1, is an open field.

Photo, circa 1950, Courtesy of Gertrude Christie, Mapleton. The Polaris as seen from the air. Those are potato fields all around.

69

BREEZY ACRES DRIVE-IN BOOTHBAY

THOSE WERE THE DAYS! was pretty much put to bed when I learned that a man named Lowell Spicer operated a drive-in in Boothbay in the 1940s. Lowell, 73, wasn't hard to find. And he wasn't hard to talk with, although I could tell he was puzzled as to why I wanted to know all about something that happened so long ago. "You sure are a persistent fellow," he commented.

Lowell named his enterprise the Breezy Acres Drive-In. "It was always breezy on that part of the (family) farm," he explains. "That part" was an open field on which Lowell fashioned a screen and a pair of speakers in the spring of 1949. Lowell was looking for something that would earn him some money. He didn't find it at the drive-in. "You paid your bills and then might have enough left over for gas and smokes," he chuckles.

Lowell's drive-in was not Radio City Music Hall. There was the field, with a capacity of 30 or so autos. There were the two speakers. There was the projection booth. Lowell built that prefab-style in Bath and then hauled it to Breezy Acres by trailer. There was no refreshment stand. "Just pictures," Lowell phrases it.

Lowell operated through Labor Day, when the "crowds" began to peter out. A month later the theatre's homemade screen blew down during a storm. Lowell figured it wasn't worth rebuilding. On the Breezy Acres' former site, just south of the Boothbay Railway Museum on Route 27, there today remains absolutely nothing from the drive-in's one season under the stars.

Cover of Grand Opening folder, June/July 1949. Courtesy of Francis and Eleanor Pickett, Westbrook. Notice the listing of the drive-in's many advantages.

Drive-Ins

STARLITE DRIVE-IN MADISON

The Starlite was the product of an adventuresome move on the part of three Gorham State Teachers College students in 1949. "We had seen one (a drive-in) someplace and it struck us as something we could do." So explains Francis Pickett, one of the three. Why Madison? "Well, we went to the state," recalls Curtis Tolman, the second of the trio, "and got a traffic map. Madison was one of the best (in terms of number of cars that passed through daily)."

The theatre opened on July 1, 1949. "The first night was packed," well recollects Francis. It turns out, though, that the Starlite's screen wasn't big enough to accommodate so large a crowd. "A lot of people couldn't see the screen very well and they left," continues Francis. "But," he adds, "after that it settled down and we had a steady crowd."

One of the steady crowd was lifelong Madison resident Leo Demchak. Leo, 76, remembers things a little differently. "They had speakers mounted on poles, which you had to lean out of your car to hear the voice of the movie." And, Leo adds quickly, "The mosquitos and black flies were horrendous. They bit the hell out of you. We smoked cigarettes one after the other to keep the bugs away."

Photo, 1949. Courtesy of Francis and Eleanor Pickett, Westbrook. Here's the Starlite's screen, looking not unlike a big tv screen. Note the star tipped onto the top. The screen was constructed entirely by the partners. Curtis said he couldn't remember for sure, but he thought it took about three or four days to complete. "Not very long," as he says.

After two seasons Francis, Curtis and the third member of the partnership, Frank Hesdorfer, Jr., decided to call it quits. As Curtis, who admits "the mosquitos were not good," puts it, "We didn't lose money but we didn't make a lot, either. And we could make more (money) doing something else." On the theatre's old site on Lakewood Road there are now two auto dealerships, Sprague Dodge and People's Garage.

LEWISTON DRIVE-IN
LEWISTON

Different people in and around L/A have different memories of the Lewiston Drive-In. "I remember all the old John Waynes," grins 48-year old Lewiston native Mike Fournier. "It'd be a Friday or a Saturday and my parents would say 'We're going to the drive-in.' And off we'd go. We'd always get there early - 40-45 minutes before showtime - and my parents would take me over to the playground. This is when I was about eight, give or take, in the early 1960s. It (the theatre) was always packed."

Forget the playground: it was the food that 47-year old Mechanic Falls' native Gil Strait recalls most. Back in 1964-65, when he was eight or nine. "The food seemed really good. It was a real treat. That's because," explains Gil, "we didn't have pizza or hot dogs at home. My favorite (at the drive-in) was pizza. It wasn't very common then. Not for us anyway: we lived out in Mechanic Falls."

Forget both the playground and the food. What longtime Auburn resident Sharon Packer recalls is "the experience." She remembers watching shows with her sons in the early 1980s, enjoying what she refers to as "the mystery of the big screen and the dark car." Says Sharon: "There you are enclosed in your own little space. The car is familiar. And there's that big screen in

Ad, *Lewiston Evening Journal*, September 5, 1959. Somebody, somewhere had the idea of running movies - four or five of them - all night long on the eve of Memorial Day, the 4th of July, and Labor Day. It was a good idea and one that did very well for Maine's drive-ins.

Drive-Ins

front of you. It yields," she sums up, "an intimacy that you just don't get in a regular theatre."

The Lewiston Drive-In opened on July 1, 1949. As was the case with quite a few other drive-ins, it was advertised as "New England's Finest Outdoor Theatre." There was space for 500 cars. And, to help marshal the crowds, there were eight "traffic directors" to help patrons find an open spot and park properly. A "well-stocked snack bar" and "large, clean rest rooms" were also promised, as was a mosquito-control program to try to keep the winged critters from enjoying the show, too.

By 1985 the Lewiston Drive-In was being eyed by New Hampshire-native Bob Foss as a location for something other than movie viewing: Bob thought the site perfect for a mobile home park and sales office. He purchased the theatre in July of that year, but allowed the drive-in to finish its season. The last show ran on Labor Day, September 2nd. The theatre was then razed. On its former site, 1149 Sabattus Street, there is now Country Lane Estates and Homes. Ironically, Mike Fournier's parents own and occupy a trailer in the mobile home park. "I think it (his parents' trailer) is right where the concession stand stood. Sometimes," Mike adds, hamming it up at least a mite, " I think I can even still smell the hamburgers cooking and the popcorn popping."

AUBURN DRIVE-IN AUBURN

Think of "paired" cities in Maine and you think of Portland/South Portland, Bangor/Brewer, Biddeford/Saco. Think of "paired" drive-in cities in Maine and you think of Lewiston/Auburn: L/A had three operating drive-ins, as many as the other pairs combined. The longest lasting of the three was the Auburn Drive-In. It opened July 2, 1949 and closed July 24, 1988. That's a lot of years and a lot of shows.

The Auburn Drive-In almost also had the distinction of being L/A's first drive-in. It lost out by exactly one day to the Lewiston Drive-In. When it opened, though, it wasn't called the Auburn Drive-In. It was the Danville Drive-In, the dream-come-true for a couple of Vermonters, Warren Collins and Robert Wood. The two had been in the Army Air Corps during World War II. Collins, in fact, had been shot down over Germany and had spent considerable time as a POW. The *Lewiston Evening Journal*, in an article on the coming of the drive-in, noted that Warren's dad, Ray Collins, had been a southpaw pitcher for the Red Sox for seven seasons,* several of them just before WWI when Lewiston's own Bill Carrigan was Bosox manager.

Collins and Wood made a classic mistake: they

tried to run their drive-in long distance from Vermont. It didn't work. Within a year they'd sold to Lockwood & Gordon, Inc., a firm that owned the Lewiston Drive-In and others around the state. When the theatre re-opened on June 21, 1950 it had a new name - the Auburn Drive-In - as well as new owners.

An Auburn native who well recalls the Auburn Drive-In is 55-year old Susan (Brock) Gordon. "I can remember seeing KING KONG," she smiles. "It was my first drive-in movie, when I was five or so. My mother and aunt took my sister and me. When the movie came on I was scared to death. Petrified," she says, smiling a little less. "On a big screen it really was intimidating."

Another "rememberer" is 34-year old Leeds native Paul Wheeler. His memories, from when he was a youngster in the mid-1970s, though, are mostly about the theatre's food. "I used to love the snack bar," he beams. "The smell of the popcorn. I couldn't wait for those dancing cartoons at intermission. The food - the bucket of popcorn and the sodas - would come dancing across the screen. They were all animated." Paul's favorites: the popcorn ("I was a big popcorn fan.") and the Ju-Jubes.

The Auburn Drive-In was closed during the season of 1986. It was then re-opened, under new management, and ran through 1987 and part of 1988. In July 1988 management gave up the ghost. "If your kids or grandkids have never been to a drive-in take them this weekend. They (drive-in movies) will never return" and "This is an End of an Era," ran ads in the *Lewiston Evening Journal* toward the end of July. The last show ran Sunday, July 24th. It *was* the end of an era.

On the drive-in's former site, on Poland Spring Road/Route 122 just off Washington Street/ Routes 4, 100 and 202, there is now a pair of mobile homes.

*The Sox could well use him now: the lefty was 19-8 one year (1913) and 20-13 the next (1914).

Ad, *Lewiston Evening Journal*, July 2, 1951. Insofar as possible I tried to select ads that I found attractive. I liked this one a lot.

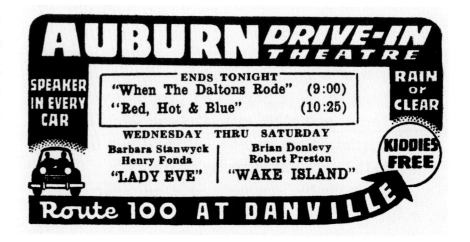

Drive-Ins

ENFIELD DRIVE-IN
ENFIELD

When it came to drive-ins in Maine the people who started them were all over the spectrum. There were sizable companies. There were mom and pops. Boston-native Sam Nyer, now 75, was probably somewhere in between. "I was selling life insurance in 1949," he told me in a January 2001 interview, "and I met a man - I forget his name - in Milbridge. He rented out 16mm films to halls and such in central and northern Maine. He was doing good. He said to me: 'You're a bright young man. Why don't you open a drive-in theatre?' I said 'What's that?' He explained they were being built all over and that families with young kids liked them and that, with the war over, there were a lot of young kids."

"So he talked me into it. I scouted out locations in Lincoln and West Enfield and decided on Enfield. I scraped up some money and did most of the work (building the theatre) myself. I put up $1,000 and owed $3,000-$4,000. Things were cheap in those days. And people who sold me lumber and stuff said 'Pay me later.' I think," concludes Sam, "that the first 50 cars that came (to the drive-in) were my creditors."

Sam's "baby" opened July 2, 1949. An opening day ad in *The Bangor Daily News* promised a large parking area, space for trucks, and seats for those people without a car. The theatre's

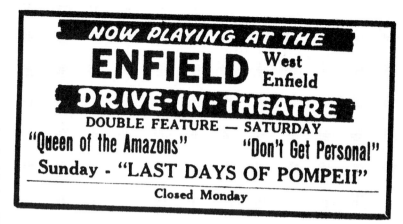

Ad, *The Bangor Daily News*, Sept. 10, 1949. Grandiose sagas the likes of THE LAST DAYS OF POMPEII and BEN HUR generally did well at drive-in box offices. Patrons liked to view something spectacular - even "educational" - during their evening under the stars.

early slogan was "Where You Drive In And Relax." On the screen was a steady diet of westerns, comedies, musicals, swashbucklers, and horror. Sometimes Sam would ham it up a little, especially with horror flicks. A good example was his "Terrorific Double Chill Show" of July 8, 1950. With GHOSTS ON THE LOOSE and SPOOKS RUN WILD on the screen and dancing both before and after the show, how could you lose?

Sam Nyer (who also owned the drive-in in Trenton: see page 67) closed Enfield at the end of the 1985 season. "There was a lack of business," he says rather simply. "Plus it was a headache: all the repairs. And tv really began to hurt: there were much better programs than there had been."

PORTLAND DRIVE-IN
SCARBOROUGH

Jennifer Jortberg's introduction to the Portland Drive-In was fleeting. "I remember as a kid - when I was about eight or nine - driving with my parents by the Portland Drive-In, down Route 1, and my sisters and me craning our necks to see what was playing. There was a (traffic) light there, by the drive-in, and we hoped it would be red. Then," laughs Jennifer, "we could see more of the screen."

Drive-in advertising art, 1950s. In spite of the "Rain or Clear" wording, spending an evening at the drive-in on a rainy night wasn't really a whole lot of fun.

Such was (and is) the lure of the drive-in. And the Portland Drive-In had a lot that was alluring. Opened the Saturday of Independence Day weekend, 1949, the Portland was trumpeted in its ads as "New England's Finest Outdoor Theatre" and home to the "World's Largest Screen." This latter claim is hard to verify, but at 70' x 60' the theatre's screen was not in danger of being overlooked. Admission was 50¢ per person. Cars were free. So were children under 12.

The Portland Drive-In was a stellar member of Maine's drive-in line-up all through the 1950s and 1960s. It was so successful, in fact, that a second screen was added in October 1968. The Portland Drive-In became the Portland Twin Drive-In.

Another Portland innovation was in-car heaters. Dana Duhamel, who worked at the theatre from 1981 to 1985, recalls the heaters well: "They were bright red and were about $1\frac{1}{2}$ times the size of the speaker. They (the heaters) were on a separate pole, right alongside the speaker poles. They worked great. Because of the heaters we were open all year. We did so well in the winter," continues Dana, "that we had to have a Scarborough police officer to direct traffic. Even with him (the officer) there were real traffic jams. And this would be in January

Drive-Ins

Photo, October 1990. The Portland Drive-In closed in 1986, but its memorable sign lived on. Scarborough town councilor Janice Peltier tried to save it. Local sign company owner Joe Tufts agreed to help. Their efforts, however, were to no avail: the sign was demolished in March 1994.

or February. The biggest problem with the heater," Dana concludes, "was when people drove away with the speaker still in their car they drove away with the heater, too."

Eventually, of course, hard times arrived. Cable tv, vcrs, and indoor multi-plexes all took a toll. By 1986 the theatre's turnouts were sparse. In September the Portland Drive-In closed, not only for the season, but forever. The drive-in's site, on Route 1 south of Oak Hill, is now an empty lot. But remnants of the theatre's glory days are yet scattered here and there across the area. And, with a little imagination, it's not too terribly difficult to visualize 700 or so cars packed in on a summer Saturday night.

WINDHAM DRIVE-IN NORTH WINDHAM

The Windham Drive-In opened July 26, 1949. Its first showing featured RACHEL AND THE STRANGER, with Loretta Young, William Holden, and Robert Mitchum. The theatre's initial proprietor was Jimmy Spiers. "He was an entrepreneur," recalls Don Rich, who worked at the drive-in as a teenager in the early 1950s. Adds Don: "He (Jimmy) owned the Goodyear Tire store in Portland, but he knew Windham because he and his family had a cottage on Little Sebago. He was a hard

Ad, *Portland Press Herald*, July 3, 1958. You may be certain that Windham's hipsters turned out for MR. ROCK & ROLL, the story of Alan (not "Allen") Freed, the man most credited with popularizing rock 'n roll. Appearing with Alan in the film were such legends as Clyde McPhatter, Chuck Berry, the Moonglows, LaVern Baker, and Frankie Lymon & the Teenagers.

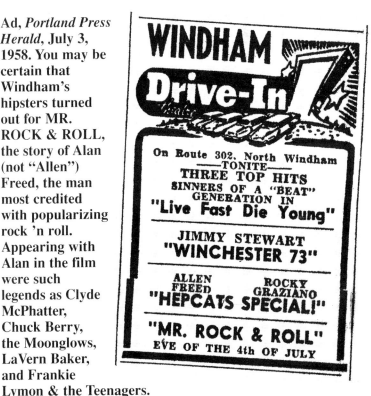

worker. Kind of a workaholic. But he loved it (the theatre)."

Don also recalls that, to start with, there was a single roof-mounted speaker. People who lived nearby could hear what was playing. They just couldn't see it. Don's job was to help people find a row and park their car. "And not take too much space," he adds.

Another ex-employee, but in the early 1960s, was Carol (Lewis) Taylor. "I did a little bit of everything," she laughs. "I was mostly in the concession stand, selling popcorn - we had an old popcorn machine that was there from the year one - pizzas, French fries, and clamcakes. The clamcakes were made right there. Big sellers were the pizzas and clamcakes, and hamburgers and hot dogs. Basic drive-in food."

Carol also well remembers the drive-in's kiddy train. "The playground had a little train that kids could ride and that went right through the pines behind the concession stand. The young kids, especially, thought it was fun."

The Windham Drive-In closed in October 1987. On its former site on Route 302 there is now a vacant lot next to Norman-David Lincoln-Mercury. "But," adds Carol in final tribute, "we still laugh and joke nowadays, if the traffic is heavy, that the drive-in must've just gotten out... because that was the only time there'd be a steady line of traffic in those days."

WINSLOW (WATERVILLE) DRIVE-IN WINSLOW

The record for the all-time shortest-lived drive-in theatre name almost certainly goes to the Waterville Drive-In. It opened on Tuesday, July 26, 1949. And closed a scant three days later, on Friday the 29th. The theatre was then almost immediately re-opened as the Winslow Drive-In. "That's (the change in name) because the people of Winslow made a stink," laughs 66-year old Winslow native Bill Pleau. "They said: 'It's in Winslow so it should be called Winslow.'"

Speaking of records, Bill was the theatre's projectionist for 32 years. That's a tough one to top. Bill had a lot of pleasant moments in those 32 years, but he had an embarrassing moment, too. "One time in the late 1950s," he recounts, "I got the reels for a movie mixed up, and a friend came into the projection booth and said 'There's something wrong.' Well, I looked out and said 'It looks good to me. What's wrong?' And he said, 'Bill, look at that guy there (pointing to a man in the movie). He was killed a while back... and now he's back alive.' And then the horns started blowing. So I made an announcement and then re-ran (the correct reel). Most people," Bill laughs now, "thought it was funny."

Drive-Ins

Ad, *Morning Sentinel*,
July 29, 1949

Ad, *Morning Sentinel*,
August 4, 1949

Now you see it. Now you don't. You had to have been quick to have attended the Waterville Drive-In: it lasted but four days, from July 25, 1949 to July 29, 1949. Its name was then changed to the Winslow Drive-In.

During what he calls "The Golden Years," Bill remembers a lot of full parking lots. "In the fifties we refused cars almost every Saturday night. We were full-up." But Bill also remembers toward the end when one evening he ran the show for a grand total of two cars. "The show must go on," as he says.

The Winslow Drive-In closed after its showing of September 1, 1986. As management's way of saying thanks, the first 100 cars to show up on each of the final three nights received an old in-car speaker.

The drive-in is long gone now. But Bill Pleau yet remembers: "I loved the people. And the kids in the playground. All the activity. I'd walk around (before the show) and talk to people. I knew everybody and everybody knew me. It was fun."

Photos, May 1985. Courtesy of Myrtle McKenna/Rumford Historical Society, Rumford. Pictured are the theatre's ticket booth and a pair of speakers during their last year of existence. "What amazed everyone," remarks Nelson Mahar, "was how often people would drive off with the speaker still in their car."

Drive-Ins

RUMFORD DRIVE-IN
RUMFORD

The Rumford Drive-In opened on October 5th 1949, which is pretty much the time of year when most Maine drive-ins were closed or closing. That's because construction of the 500-car capacity theatre didn't begin until late July. The theatre was built by local movie house mogul - he owned "hardtop" theatres in Rumford, Auburn, and Mexico - Edmund G. Pollard. Total cost was estimated to be $150,000.

Nelson Mahar, the *electrician* for the project, remembers the *carpenters* on the job were paid more as the screen they were erecting got higher. They started at $1.25 an hour and rose to $3.25 when they reached the very top, 90 feet (the distance between home and first at Hadlock or Fenway: not a recommended distance to fall) off the ground. Nelson got to set up spotlights at the top of that same screen... but for $1.15 per hour and no increase with the height.

The Rumford Drive-In ran for 36 seasons. By the 36th, 1985, patrons were scarce. It was also estimated the theatre needed $30,000 in renovations. The drive-in limped along - open weekends only - until the end of the season. It then closed for good, and was completely dismantled in May 1986. On the site, off Route 2 in East Rumford, there is today an empty lot.

SANFORD DRIVE-IN
SANFORD

After his two years at the helm of the Naples Drive-In (q.v.), Russell Martin shifted his operations to Sanford. To the Sanford Drive-In. The theatre's Gala Opening ad, on May 4, 1950, played up "Latest In-Car Speakers," "Modern Refreshment Stand," and "Bottle Warming Service For Babies." On the screen on opening day, Sunday May 7th, was Edmund O'Brien and Robert Stack in FIGHTER SQUADRON, plus a cartoon and a second feature entitled VARIETY TIME.

As it turns out, Russell Martin's stay at the Sanford Drive-in was to be but a year longer than his stay at the Naples Drive-In. As Russell's daughter Sharon explains it: "The family story goes that in 1952 drive-in-chain owner E.M. Loew came to town and told Russell that he either sold the Sanford Drive-In to him, or he would build a bigger drive-in down the road!" Whether the family story is 100% on the mark is unknown. But it is known that spring 1953 ads heralded the Sanford Drive-In as now "Under the Management of E.M. Loew's Theatres." It is also known that by that very spring of 1953, Russell Martin was up and running with his newest contribution to Maine outdoor movie-going, the Cornish Drive-In (q.v.).

Under E.M. Loew management the Sanford Drive-In operated until September 1971. People recall that it was small. That the mosquitos were bad. That theatre personnel would drive around in a pick-up truck and spray in an effort to make them less bad. Mike Allaire, who used to go to the theatre on dates as a teenager, describes the sound quality as "ugh." Bea (Lantagne) Hill remembers that you could drive onto a side street and see, but not hear, the movie. Or, you could sneak in through the woods that surrounded the theatre. "We all did that," she admits with a smile.

Nowadays the woods are gone. So, too, is the drive-in. Its old site, on Main Street/Route 109, is occupied by the Breary Farms apartment complex.

BRUNSWICK DRIVE-IN BRUNSWICK

There are 409 towns in Maine that have had no drive-in. There are 39 towns that have had one. There are three towns that have had two. There was Lewiston. Caribou. And Brunswick. Brunswick was the first to go double. Both of its drive-ins opened in 1950, with the Brunswick the pacesetter. Its opening was May 26, 1950. On the screen were two Technicolor features, UNTAMED BREED and GIVE MY REGARDS TO BROADWAY, and two color cartoons. Capacity was 500 cars. Shows were changed three times a week. Admission was 50¢ per person with kids under 12 admitted free.

"Bring The Kiddies" was an early slogan. A lot of people did. Recalls Woolwich-native Paul Berry, 79: "It was a chance to get out of the house for a night. You couldn't take kids to a regular movie. But you could to a drive-in. You could go as you were. You didn't have to dress up. And the kids especially liked it." As Paul also remembers: "They (the drive-in) had a big screen and a small refreshment stand. And (individual) speakers that worked most of the time. But sometimes," he laughs, "we'd get settled and then we'd have to move."

Another who remembers is 61-year old Richmond-native Dave Trask. What he recalls is

Drive-Ins

Ad, *Bath-Brunswick Times Record,* June 2, 1983. When crosstown rival Bowdoin closed at the end of the 1982 season, Brunswick management tried to capitalize on it. It didn't work. By the end of the 1984 season Brunswick, too, was "Closed Forever."

the old hide-and-get-in-free routine. Dave's version utilized hay. "I recall hiding in the hay in the back of a pick-up truck. We did it a few times. Three or four. We were just a bunch of kids trying to see if we could get away with not having to pay. Back then," notes Dave, "that was the height of criminal mischief."

The Brunswick Drive-In eventually ran into the problems that killed so many drive-ins; its last show was on September 7, 1984. Its former site, on Route 1 heading toward Freeport, is today an empty field.

BANGOR DRIVE-IN BANGOR

When a drive-in shows its last show and closes it's just about always a private affair. There is no "obituary" in the local newspaper. And, unless theatre management decides to run "An End of an Era" ad , there is no notice of any kind. Not so with the Bangor Drive-In when it closed on July 23, 1985. *Bangor Daily News'* scribe A. Jay Higgins saw to that. He penned, in fact, not one, but two goodbyes.

Jay's initial article, headlined "Bangor Drive-In's 'magic lantern' lights screen for last time," appeared in the *BDN's* July 26, 1985 issue. On page one, no less. Wrote Jay: "Without fanfare or advance notice, the Bangor Drive-In closed its gates to the young families and romantic couples who once flocked to outer Hammond Street for the shows that ran 'from dusk until midnight." Jay then went on to share the discussion he'd had with Cinema Centers Corp., the Boston-based firm that ran the drive-in. It turned out that Cinema Centers was on the verge of opening the Bangor Mall Cinema, an eight-theatre multiplex indoor operation. So shutting down the drive-in was a question of out with the old and in with the new. In his "Talk Of The Town" column five days later, Jay termed the theatre's demise a "tragedy." After recounting how he'd "spent more than one or two

Ad, *The Bangor Daily News*, June 7, 1950. When the Bangor Drive-In opened it opened with flair. And a difficult-to-miss ad.

★ *Gala Opening Tonight* ★ ★ ★
★ WEDNESDAY, JUNE 7th ★
★ BANGOR DRIVE-IN-THEATRE ★
OUTER HAMMOND ST.

GRAND OPENING PROGRAM
DOUBLE FEATURE

"YOU'RE MY EVERYTHING"	"RUSTY SAVES A LIFE"
In Technicolor With DAN DAILEY and ANN BAXTER	Starring TED DONALDSON Also 2 COLOR CARTOONS

★ First Season of Movies Under the Stars ★

INDIVIDUAL SPEAKER FOR EACH CAR
YOU ADJUST THE VOLUME TO SUIT YOUR OWN TASTE

★ NO BABY SITTER PROBLEM
You can now take the children with you, have them under your own watchful eye.

★ NO MORE PARKING WORRIES
You can now enjoy the show in the comfort of your own car.

★ FINEST R. C. A. SOUND
★ SHOW STARTS AT DUSK

Refreshment Stand, Popcorn and Cold Drinks

ADMISSION ADULTS
50c TAX INC.
CHILDREN UNDER 12 FREE
BOX OFFICE OPENS
AT 6 P. M.

Free bottle warming service. Bring the children to the show.

CONTINUOUS DUSK UNTIL MIDNIGHT

Drive-Ins

evenings jousting for a prime spot in the sought-out seventh row," Jay lamented his concern. Not for himself, but for "the untold generations of little Bangorians to come. They will never know that their city once had a drive-in."

The Bangor Drive-In opened on June 7, 1950. An article in The *BDN* stated the theatre cost an estimated $100,000 to build and that it "boasts every modern improvement yet devised for establishments of its type." Approximately 140 tons of concrete and steel were said to have been used to support the huge 65' x 70' screen, a screen, incidentally, that was able to withstand winds of up to 100 miles per hour. More of a problem than high winds, however, was the theatre's neighbor, Harold D. Johnson. Less than a year after the drive-in's opening, Johnson built a slew of pens and stocked them with pigs. The result: smells that were described as "terrible," "foul," "nauseating," and "rotten." Needless to say, said pigs were not conducive to business at the drive-in. Eventually the "Piggery Problem" was resolved, but it led to few laughs among drive-in hierarchy for most of 1951 and over half of 1952.

The Bangor Drive-In has been closed for close to two decades now, but both of the theatre's screens - the drive-in was twinned in July 1978 - yet stand tall on outer Hammond Street, appearing not unlike a pair of giant tombstones.

Ad, *The Bangor Daily News*, July 2, 1954. You might very well ask yourself who would pay good money to see the likes of B-GIRL RHAPSODY. The answer: so many patrons that theatre management held B-GIRL over for a second night.

85

Ad, *The Bangor Daily News*, June 7, 1952. For a small town Milo was big when it came to movie theatres. There was, of course, the drive-in, in operation from 1950 to 1974. But there was also, from 1913 to 1962, the Chic (called the Milo Theatre from 1932 until its closing) Theatre, pronounced "Chick" and located in the heart of town.

MILO DRIVE-IN
MILO

It happened in Milo. Dick Shaw, son of Ward Shaw (see page 34), tells the story of the time his grandmother and stepgrandfather made their first visit to a drive-in. Since the couple lived in Milo the visit was made, not surprisingly, to the Milo Drive-In. "They," chuckles Dick, "sat in their car throughout the movie and remarked to friends the next day that 'It was the damnedest thing, paying good money to see a movie without any sound.' Their friends tactfully told them to roll down their windows the next time and attach the metal speaker."

The Milo Drive-In opened on Saturday, June 10, 1950, just weeks before E.M. Loew's Bangor-Brewer Drive-In in Brewer. In ads in *The Bangor Daily News* both made the usual grandiose claims. Bangor-Brewer was touted as "New England's Largest and Most Beautiful Drive-In Theatre" while Milo was "Your Newest, Most Modern Evening Entertainment." Milo's ad, however, was a winner with respect to those all-important creature comforts: its ad promised "Handy Refreshment Stand" and "Convenient Rest Room." If that weren't enough, it also promised a modern nursery and, among the first in Maine, bottle warmers in the nursery. On the screen, as if it really mattered to most people, there was a pair of Technicolor features, ALBUQUERQUE (starring Randolph Scott, Barbara Britton, and everybody's favorite, George "Gabby" Hayes) and ADVENTURE ISLAND (with Rory Calhoun and Rhonda Fleming).

Drive-Ins

The proprietors of the drive-in for its first dozen years were Walter and Ella Mills. Its proprietors for its last dozen years were Paul and Jane Treworgy, who took over in 1962. "Business was good in the '60s," Jane recalls. Although, as she notes, at 75¢ apiece admission she and Paul weren't really raking in the big bucks. What Jane is proudest of was that, with a crew of three, she could get 600 people through the snack bar in 20 minutes. "Wouldn't McDonald's like to have that crew!" she beams.

After the sixties came the seventies. "They were a poor time for the drive-in business," laments Jane. Movie rental fees were high, plus there was the constant need to advertise. By 1974 the Treworgys decided they'd had enough. The last show was September 22nd. As Allen Monroe, who used to hang out at the drive-in with Paul and Jane's son John and daughter Susan, puts it: "It seemed like the end of an era. It was sad that our town wouldn't have it (the drive-in) as an entertainment outlet any longer."

The old drive-in yet stands, albeit vandalized, on Route 155 outside of town. "Paul still has some films stored away in case we open again," says Jane. But then she quickly, very quickly, adds "That's a joke!"

YARMOUTH DRIVE-IN
YARMOUTH

Finding people in Yarmouth who recall the Yarmouth Drive-In wasn't easy. First of all, the Yarmouth closed a lot sooner - 1962 - than most of its contemporaries. Second of all, it seemed like everyone I asked who was old enough to have remembered was from "away." There are a lot of transplants in Yarmouth.

One person who does remember is Mary Estelle Blake. But Mary Estelle, arguably Yarmouth's most colorful citizen, doesn't remember a whole lot. Just the basics. That it was there. That some people would go: "because they didn't have anything else to do. There was a canteen and you could get popcorn and food. It was," sums up Mary Estelle succinctly, "an evening's entertainment."

Elinor (Richards) Jones has far more extensive memories. She remembers the drive-in as a popular hangout for kids. "I don't recall any adults going," she laughs, adding "I know my parents never went."

Autos were in short supply during Elinor's North Yarmouth Academy teenage years in the early 1950s. But Elinor had a friend who had a Studebaker. Actually it was her friend's parents' Studebaker, but she was allowed to use it. "We'd all go with her," Elinor thinks back. "The car would be all piled high with kids." There was no socializing following the show,

YARMOUTH DRIVE - IN THEATRE

DRIVE-IN KEEP COOL

Fri. and Sat.   Aug. 25-26
Terry Moore and Van Johnson
in
"MIGHTY JOE YOUNG"
— also —
TIM HOLT
in
"THE STAGE COACH KID"
Plus Two Color Cartoons
Open 7:30; Show Starts at Dusk
Adm. 50c Tax Inc.
Children under 12 Free

Sun.-Mon.-Tues. - Aug. 27-28-29
Kirk Douglass-Marilyn Maxwell
in
"THE CHAMPION"
— also —
Fred MacMurray
in
"DON'T TRUST YOUR
HUSBAND"
Plus Two Color Cartoons
Open 7:30; Show Starts at Dusk
Adm. 50c Tax Inc.
Children under 12 Free

Wed. and Thurs.   Aug. 30-31
Robert Michum-William Bendix
in
"THE BIG STEAL"
— also —
Michael O'Shea
in
"THE THREAT"
Plus Two Color Cartoons
Open 7:30; Show Starts at Dusk
Adm. 50c Tax Inc.
Children under 12 Free

Ad, *Talk of the Towns* newspaper, August 25, 1950. Courtesy of Yarmouth Historical Society. In the days before almost universal air conditioning, nature's way of air cooling - being outside - was a summertime drive-in selling point.

P.S. In this ad there are two well known old-time actors with misspelled last names. Can you identify them? For answer turn upside down.

Answer: Kirk Douglass should be Kirk Douglas and Robert Michum should be Robert Mitchum.

however. "We all had to be home 15 minutes after the theatre closed," laughs Elinor again. "How did the parents know when the theatre closed?" I asked. "Parents knew everything in those days," she answered.

The Yarmouth Drive-In, touted as "one of the most modern of its type in Maine" by *The Brunswick Record*, opened on June 14, 1950. Its owner/operator was Lewis Packard of Brunswick. The drive-in hummed along, doing what drive-ins do, through the 1950s. Nobody recalls anything distinctive about it. Its greatest moment of glory may have come after the '58 season when someone put "We Had To Close Before We Froze" on the drive-in's signboard.

Along about 1959 local businessman Ed Dakin bought the theatre… and ended up closing it three years later, after the Labor Day weekend show of 1962. Longtime Yarmouth resident Walter Zimont's feeling is that Dakin had a number of other interests and that he may have felt spread too thin. Walter also recalls that business had fallen off. The drive-in stood vacant for a number of years before being leveled for what is now a Shop 'n Save shopping center.

Drive-Ins

E.M. LOEW'S BANGOR-BREWER DRIVE-IN BREWER

What would you guess has been the most used name in Maine movie theatre annals? Was it Bijou? No. Was it State or Strand? Quite possibly. But I'd put my money on E.M. Loew's.

E. (Elias) M. Loew was born in Austria in 1898 and came to America when he was 13, in 1911. He settled in Boston. Correctly sensing the tremendous growth potential of the motion picture industry, Loew bought his first theatre, the old Crystal Theatre in Worcester, in 1916 when he was still a teenager. His second acquisition was the Capitol in Lynn, Massachusetts. His third, the Portland Theatre, on Preble Street, in Portland. Before he was through the man that *Variety* would label "a pioneer showman" owned 70 hardtop theatres, 17 "ozoners," and six hotels and nightclubs, including the famed Latin Quarter nightspots in New York and Miami. Loew (no relation to Marcus Loew, the founder of MGM and proprietor of the Loew's Theatre chain) owned at least six Maine theatres, scattered from Wells Beach (see page 17) to Brewer, at one time or another. Three of those were drive-ins, in Sanford, Manchester (Augusta), and, of course, Brewer. E.M. Loew died, at age 86, in October 1984. His estate was estimated to be worth $50,000,000.

E.M. Loew's Bangor-Brewer Drive-In opened on the Fourth of July, 1950. It was advertised as yet another "New England's Largest and Finest" complete with "World's Largest Screen." What *was* impressive was that E.M. sprang for a huge, almost full page, ad in *The Bangor Daily News* to herald the grand event. It was, perhaps, "The World's Largest Drive-

Ad, *The Bangor Daily News*, August 3, 1958. Dick Shaw of Bangor recalls going to the Bangor-Brewer Drive-In for a cartoon feature as a kid and having to share the good seats with the bad. It seems the Shaws' old Plymouth had a metal band down the middle of the front window, making for visibility that was less than desired. "We children (Dick, his brother, and his sister) took turns sitting in the middle of the front - i.e., the 'bad' seat" - he still remembers after all these many years.

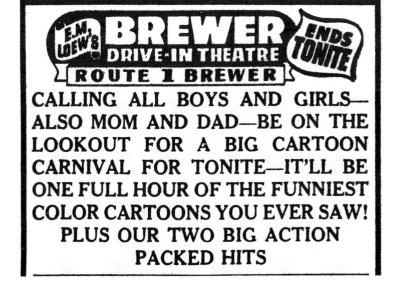

In *Ad!*" On the screen were "2 Mighty Technicolor Triumphs," ALI BABA AND THE FORTY THIEVES, and, with a "Cast Of Thousands," THE PHANTOM OF THE OPERA.

Through its many years, E.M. Loew's Bangor-Brewer Drive-In featured all that was expected from a drive-in... and more. There was a large playground, a well-stocked concession stand, a bottle-warming service, dusk-to-dawn shows, cartoon carnivals. Plus there was, off and on, live entertainment (Jack Wunderlich and his WGUY Disc Jockey Program "Playing Your Favorite Recordings As You Request Them" was a regular) and "Adults Only" shows (such as BATHING BEAUTY CAPERS, starring Sutira, the body beautiful.).

Eventually, as with so many other drive-ins, business turned sour. Patrons stopped requesting songs. Patrons stopped drooling over Sutira. Patrons stopped being patrons. Operations came to an end in 1986. In May 1987 the once rather grandiose theatre was demolished as a safety precaution. It seems sections of the theatre were falling down. The drive-in's former site, on Wilson Street/Route 1A, is now an overgrown field.

KENNEBUNK DRIVE-IN KENNEBUNK

"My father, James ('Jimmy'), was in the Navy in World War II and when he got out of the service he thought drive-in theatres were going to be the coming thing." So explains J.P. Nadeau, Jimmy's son, as to why his dad, a native of Dover, New Hampshire, involved himself in three drive-ins across two states.

Actually, it took seven years for Jimmy's dream to materialize. By 1952, however, he was ready to make the big move. He took his accumulated savings, mortgaged as much as he could, and convinced his brother Michael to go in with him. Jimmy's first theatre was the Sunset Drive-In in Rochester, New Hampshire. Then, a year or so later, came the Newington Drive-In, located in Newington, New Hampshire. In 1957 Jimmy made his way across the border, purchasing the seven-year-old Kennebunk Drive-In in Kennebunk.

Most of J.P.'s memories of his dad's drive-in years revolve around the burden of getting movies to show. Details J.P.: "You had to bid for movies. Go to Boston and bid. And if you wanted a big movie like BEN HUR you might end up having to also take 10 B or C movies, too. It," J.P. still says bitterly, "was oppressive." J.P. is proud, though, that his father stood up to the system, and that he was instrumental in getting a more equitable set of practices put into effect.

Drive-Ins

Poster, 1970. Drive-ins, as with "hardtops," showed some movies that were better than others. MYRA BRECKINRIDGE was not one of these. In his HALLIWELL'S FILM GUIDE, movie critic Leslie Halliwell termed the controversial sex-change movie "sleazy and aimless." Did Mr. Halliwell like co-feature JUSTINE any better? Nope. He called it "disastrous" and "like a bad rehearsal for a film."

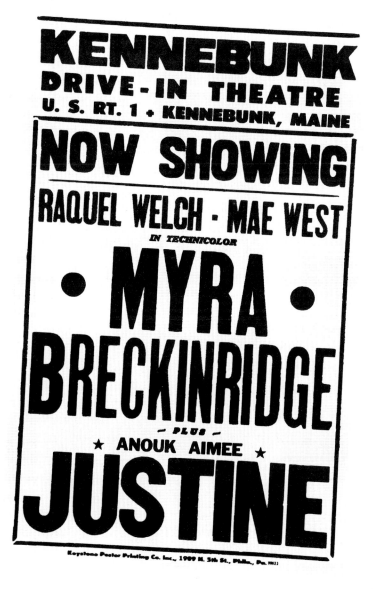

On the lighter side is 45-year old Leslie Lindgren's remembrance. Leslie resided in Boston as a youth, but she had relatives in Kennebunk... relatives who lived near the drive-in. Leslie's cousin Jimmy had a friend who lived even closer. And the friend had constructed a tree house with a direct line of vision to the theatre's screen. "When we came up to visit during the summer," Leslie still recalls with a grin, "we'd all climb up and watch. But we couldn't hear. It was pretty cool. Like watching silent movies."

Another person who lived very near the drive-in is Jim Keating. In fact he and J.P. were comrades during their formative years, with Jim spending a lot of time at the drive-in. I was, accordingly, hopeful that Jim might have access to an old photo or two. But he doesn't. No photos. "I am afraid that like so many things," he notes somewhat wistfully, "I assumed that it would always be there."

The Kennebunk Drive-In opened July 19, 1950 and closed September 28, 1980. Its former site on U.S. Route 1 is now occupied by an office condominium complex.

AUGUSTA DRIVE-IN MANCHESTER

Long-time E.M. Loew's Augusta Drive-In logo. When I asked my wife Catherine, an Augusta native, if she and her Cony friends called the theatre "E.M Loew's" or "Augusta," she said "We just called it the drive-in." Makes sense.

One of my favorite drive-in stories comes via Chelsea-native Gerry Cameron. Gerry, now 66, was the maintenance man at the Augusta Drive-in from the late sixties through the late seventies. "I was," as he says, "there (at the theatre) when nobody else was. From 4:00 to 10:00. A.M. I'd clean up, fix broken speakers, that sort of thing. It's amazing what you'd find that people had lost. Wallets. Watches. And, yes, underwear and bras. Like they had just fallen off."

But none of that is Gerry's finest recollection. This is: "My strangest experience came one morning around 1970. I noticed a man and a woman. I hadn't noticed them or their car. They just were suddenly there. So I walked over and asked if they'd lost something. They both acted kind of sheepish. The man said his girlfriend had thrown a hamburger wrapper out of the car window the night before and her diamond ring had come off. He said 'We were parked by the speaker over there.' And that was 60-70 feet from where they were looking. I asked why they were looking over here when they'd been parked over there. He said 'It might have bounced.' I think they'd had a fight and she'd thrown it out of the car. Whatever, they never did find the ring." Gerry and I laughed along together as he told that story.

The Augusta Drive-In (full name: E.M. Loew's Augusta Drive-In. See page 89 for information on Mr. Loew) opened for business August 4, 1950. A large ad in the *Kennebec Journal* proclaimed the theatre to be New England's "Largest and Finest Drive-In Theatre." On the big screen was a Maria Montez (Maria was an

Drive-Ins

"exotic" Hollywood leading lady who would die in 1951) twinbill, WHITE SAVAGE and COBRA WOMAN. The ad touted the pair as "2-Mighty Technicolor Triumphs." On hand for the opening festivities were numerous civic leaders plus Beverly the Prairie Sweetheart, and Stef Campana and his orchestra. Even E.M. Loew showed up. An article in the *KJ* boasted that the drive-in (which was actually located on Route 202 in Manchester) possessed the world's largest screen, a parking lot that would accommodate 750 cars, and a playground deluxe. Randolph-native Frances Galvani recalls both the screen ("It was very high and very wide. It just set right up there.") and, especially, the playground. That it had swings, a sandbox, a teeter-totter. "The kids would have lots of fun," states Frances. "Even when the movie was on."

The theatre's last manager, Dot Belanger, 75, recalls how a group of the employees would gather together for a pot luck supper and "social hour" before the show started. And how the theatre did a land-office business with THE LOVE BUG, with "two great big lines of cars all the way back to Augusta." But Dot also recalls that business fell off in the 1980s and that J & S Oil made theatre management a very good offer for the land. Management accepted. The Augusta Drive-In's last show ran September 30, 1984.

BOWDOIN DRIVE-IN BRUNSWICK

Nowadays we have "designer" fashions and "designer" perfume. In 1950 we had a "designer" drive-in theatre. The Bowdoin Drive-In, in Brunswick. It was created by one Eugene Boragine, described in *The Brunswick Record* of the day as a "distinguished New York City designer and interior decorator." The article, in the May 11th edition of the paper, went on to state that Mr. Boragine had recently designed an amazing 52 theatres in a single year. He was, as well, said to have "designed many restaurants and clubs in New York City, including the famous Latin Quarter." Indeed, when the drive-in opened, on August 11, 1950, it was heralded as "beautiful."

Some people, as it turns out, were more bedazzled by the Bowdoin's beauty than others. One who *was* impressed - as least vis-a-vis the nearby Brunswick Drive-In - is Brunswick-native Jayne Palmer. Jayne remembers the Bowdoin as "really fancy and spacious." And, in comparison with the Brunswick, "much more high-tech looking; sleek; smooth; Hollywood looking." Jayne's recall dates back to the Bowdoin's formative years, 1950-1955, when she was a teenager at Brunswick High. "My memories are that everybody went and you'd all park in the same row or two. It'd be a warm summer night; everybody had their windows

Ad, *The Bath Daily Times*, May 22, 1953. An adventure movie paired with a musical was just about always a safe bet, bound to please most everyone. If this ad's artwork looks familiar it's because it had earlier been used by the Brunswick Drive-In (see page 55). Such art was "stock art," usable by anyone and everyone with the money to pay for it.

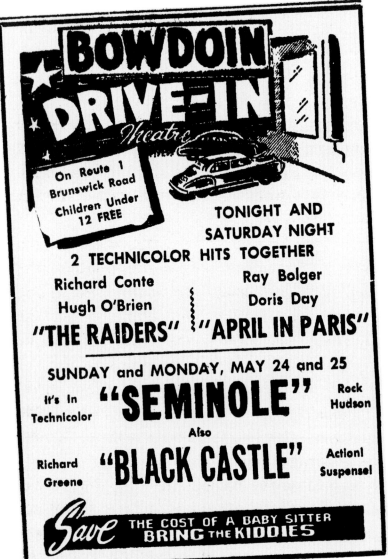

open; everybody socialized. Then we'd sneak around to see who was dating who and who was making out with who instead of watching the movie."

Jumping ahead a quarter of a century, to the late 1970s, we find longtime Brunswick resident Paul D'Alessandro less enthralled. He recalls that the grass wouldn't always be mowed and that the "ramps" that aimed each car upward for viewing purposes were often uneven. One side of the ramp - and, therefore, the car - would be higher than the other. As he puts it: "It felt kind of funny. Like there's no flat land here."

Inbetween Jayne and Paul comes Pete Fullerton. Pete, a native of Bath, went to the drive-in every couple of weeks during his Morse High years in the late 1960s. His recall is of the food: "The food was pretty bad stuff. There it was sitting under the hot lamp. It might've been there for days for all we knew.

On the other hand, however," Pete says in summation, "if you were taking a date you really didn't care much about the food. As a 17-year old with hormones kicking in you weren't too much worried about the aesthetics of the place."

Three different decades. Three different people. Three different views.

The Bowdoin Drive-In showed its last movie October 2, 1982. On its former site, on the Bath Road north of the Cooks Corner section of Brunswick, there is now an Ames discount store.

Drive-Ins

MADAWASKA DRIVE-IN FRENCHVILLE

It's appropriate that what Lorraine Pelletier recalls most fondly about her Madawaska Drive-In days is the French fries. It's appropriate (A) because the Madawaska Drive-In was actually in Frenchville, and (B) because, it was definitely in potatoland as well. Lorraine: "The biggest seller in the canteen was our French fries. On the weekends we used to go to work at 6:00 P.M. in order to be ready for the 9:00 P.M. show. We needed all that time to peel four to five barrels of potatoes, wash them, bleach them, and cut them. There was no such thing as frozen potatoes back then. We'd sell them all. And," smiles Lorraine, "if I do say so myself, they were really good."

Another big seller at the drive-in was rain visors. "Every car would own one. They sold for $5.00," notes Lorraine as she thinks back, "but they would last for the whole summer." Another standby was a product called PIC. "It drove away the mosquitos," chuckles Lorraine. "They were 10¢ a tray. People put them on their dashboard and they would last a couple of hours."

The Madawaska Drive-In was opened in 1950 by Emile Michard. A dozen years later, in 1962, it was purchased by Raoul Chasse. The screen had fallen down, but Raoul's son-in-law, Rosaire Pelletier, rebuilt it in the spring of 1963. Rosaire also enlarged it, to 52' high by 80' wide. From 1963 to 1969 Rosaire and his wife Lorraine (she of French fries and rain visor memories) leased and operated the theatre. "The drive-in was at its peak in those days," fondly recalls Lorraine. "We'd have lines of cars for miles waiting to get in to see such shows as THE TEN COMMANDMENTS. Young boys who were enterprising would walk from car to car before the show and ask the occupants if they wanted their windshield washed for a tip. It was surprising how much money they would make in an evening and it was theirs to keep."

Lorraine's favorite story from those golden years: "I remember one time my mother was working as cashier and someone wanted a bag of chips. She had us in stitches when she repeatedly asked for a bag of *plain* barbeque chips."

In 1969 the drive-in was sold. And then again after that. It was closed after the season of 1986 and dismantled two years later to make way for a self-storage facility.

Note: for more on the Pelletiers and their drive-in doings in the Madawaska area please see pages see 130 and 131, and for more on the Madawaska Drive-in please see the next page.

The front and back of the Madawaska Drive-In's 52' high/80' wide screen. The "back side" photo is from 1987, toward the end of the screen's days. The "front side" shot is circa 1966. That's Rosaire, looking like a giant bug, painting the screen. "It took Rosaire three days at eight hours a day to paint the screen," recounts Lorraine. "He used a four-inch paintbrush. It was quite a job but he enjoyed it. It had to be painted every three years. He constructed a box-shaped platform with cable hoists to go up and down. It's a good thing he wasn't afraid of heights. I was the one that was afraid for him. The view from up there was beautiful. He" sums up Lorraine, "didn't consider painting the screen a hard job, just a long one." Photo courtesy of Lorraine Pelletier, Madawaska.

Drive-Ins

VAN BUREN DRIVE-IN
VAN BUREN

Dayton Grandmaison sums up the joy of an evening at the drive-in about as well as anybody. "It was," he says, "such a complete experience: your family and/or friends, great movies, great food, the moon and the stars. In the 1950s and 1960s," continues Dayton, "we could play anything at the drive-in as long as it was a halfway decent movie and we hadn't already played it."

The Van Buren Drive-In opened in the late summer of 1950. Its first proprietor was Lillian G. Keegan, a locally-successful businesswoman who wanted to be part of the drive-in boom. She is reported to have spent $100,000 on the theatre's construction. Mrs. Keegan also owned the highly profitable Gayety, a "regular" movie theatre in downtown Van Buren. In 1961 she ran headlong into financial difficulties and sold both theatres to Madaswaska-native O'Neil Cyr. Cyr changed the drive-in's name to the Cyr Drive-In and operated it for the season of 1961. He then leased the drive-in to Dayton's father, Gilman Grandmaison. Gilman changed the name back to the Van Buren Drive-In; purchased the theatre in 1966; operated it until its finale in 1989.

Dayton, who worked with his dad at the theatre, smiles as he remembers a movie entitled THE OUTER SPACE CONNECTION. Dayton recalls cars being driven in three abreast - in what was a two-lane entranceway - for that one. "And we did phenomenally well with SATURDAY NIGHT FEVER," grins Dayton. "The poster (for the film) was stolen the night it was posted. That was usually a good indication that interest in a particular movie was high, and that attendance would be good." ("Unless," adds Dayton, "*all* of the posters disappeared. That meant it was either prom night or graduation night at the local high school. It - swiping the posters - was almost an annual ritual.").

There was, however, a tremendous array of films that did not do well. And this was increasingly the case as years went by, until the final season in 1989. "The economy in our area had been slowing down for years," laments Dayton. "Business at the drive-in had been decreasing annually since about 1981. Attendance in 1987, 1988, and 1989 was terrible. We were lucky to get 30 cars a night. Twenty was normal." In addition to the usual problem of cable tv, satellite dishes, vcrs, and video rental outlets, the Van Buren Drive-In suffered from a loss of local population plus increases in the Canadian exchange rate. "Canadians were a *major* chunk of our customer base," concludes Dayton.

97

Waiting for evening to arrive. Photo, late summer, 1950. Courtesy of Dayton Grandmaison, Van Buren.

Drive-Ins

ROCKLAND DRIVE-IN
ROCKPORT

Owls Head native Jean Young recalls the Rockland Drive-In very clearly. As well she should. It's where her (now) husband proposed to her in 1966. "It was my birthday, May 3rd," remembers Jean. "During intermission my boyfriend went to the snack bar. When he came back he handed the food to me and then he reached into the glove compartment and took out a beautiful all-black velvet box. Then we switched: he held the food and I held the box. He said 'Open it.' And there was a ring. He said 'Will you marry me?' I," continues Jean, "started to cry and he got very nervous. He thought I was going to refuse him. Then I said 'Yes' and he was so relieved."

The Rockland Drive-In opened for business on June 22, 1951. Ads in the *Rockland Courier-Gazette*, not surprisingly, heralded the theatre as "Maine's Most Modern Drive-In." Jean Young doesn't much recall those early years, but she remembers well the later ones, when she was an "older" youngster. "The drive-in was the only way my parents could go out for a date. There were five of us kids. They'd (Jean's parents) throw a bunch of blankets in the back seat and tell us to go to sleep so they could watch the movie. We had a great big car - a

Buick - and it fit a lot of children. My brothers and sisters, who were younger, would snuggle up and go to sleep," relays Jean. "But I," and here she smiles a big smile, "didn't (go to sleep). I was the oldest. I got to watch the movie."

The Rockland Drive-In played 36 seasons before its final season. Its last show - at $5.00 a carload - was KARATE KID II and ST. ELMO'S FIRE on August 31, 1986. The drive-in's former site, on Route 1 at the Rockport-Camden line, is now occupied by a nursery called Plants Unlimited.

LISBON DRIVE-IN
LEWISTON

The Lisbon Drive-In opened June 6, 1952, the last of Lewiston/Auburn's three drive-ins to appear. Grand Opening ads ballyhood the usual drive-in strengths: "The Best In Movies"/ "Enjoyment For The Whole Family"/"Modern In-Car Speakers" (featuring "RCA Futuramic Dual Channel Sound") and "Ultra Modern Canteen and Snack Bar." There were also free pony rides "for all the kiddies." Some of these strengths - pony rides, for instance - faded away as the drive-in matured. Many people around L/A, in fact, best recall the Lisbon Drive-In for its "Adult Entertainment" in the 1970s and 1980s. Others, however, best recall it for its earlier, more-innocent days. One such person is longtime Lewiston resident Juliette Gallant, 63. "It (the Lisbon Drive-In) was great," beams Juliette. "You could bring your family and your own popcorn and soft drinks. I used to make a big jug of Koolaid. Strawberry or black cherry. And," she continues, "back then - in the mid-sixties - they had movies with a story. There was no killing. You could bring your family and enjoy the show together without any violence or sexual acts. Plus," she adds, "they had comics (cartoons). My husband and kids loved those."

Juliette even recalls the very last movie she saw at the Lisbon. It was Doris Day and David Niven in PLEASE DON'T EAT THE DAISIES, around 1966. Asked if it was good, she beams again. "Yes, definitely! Doris Day was the best."

Another fan of the Lisbon Drive-In - in its infant years in the early 1950s - was Lizette "Liz" Leveille. She was but a tyke at the time, but Liz can still recall the pony rides. "I used to look forward to that (the rides) as a kid. And playing on the swings. It was a fun time to get out. And," Liz hastens to add, "you didn't notice the mosquitos as a kid."

Turning philosophical, Liz characterizes those long-ago days as a "gentler time," explaining that parents didn't have to worry about their kids playing at a place like a drive-in, even if the kids were out of sight. "There was that sense of freedom," she sums up.

And, yes, Liz did go to the Lisbon Drive-In as an adult, too. "Then the mosquitos did bother me," she chuckles.

The Lisbon Drive-In's last show was an X-rated double feature - TABOO AMERICAN STYLE and PLEASURE LANE - on September 14, 1986. Its former site, on Ross Road off Lisbon Road/Route 196, is now occupied by Central (beer) Distributors.

Drive-Ins

Longtime 1950s' Lisbon Drive-In ad art work. "Rain or Clear" sounded fine… but the "Rain" part never really was. Some drive-ins tried wiping their patron's outside windshield with a glycerine solution if it were raining or looked like it might. Others offered for sale a plastic visor that reportedly could be affixed to a car in a jiffy. Did either idea really work? Sort of.

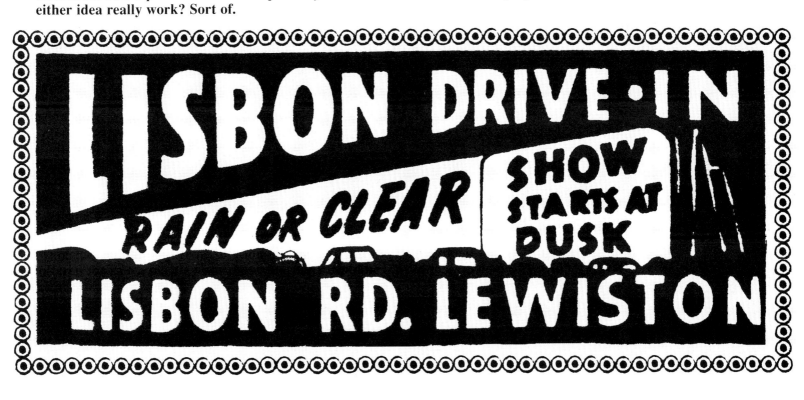

KITTERY-YORK DRIVE-IN KITTERY

There are a number of former Maine drive-in owners and/or operators who, alas, did not help out with this book at all. Not one single word. Then there's William "Willy" Dewhurst. Willy, who now resides in Nottingham, New Hampshire, typed a six-page single-spaced letter. Entitled "Some Memories of My Drive-In Days," it runs a good 4,000 words. What makes Willy's memories so interesting is that he worked up the drive-in ladder from "lot boy" (he or she who picks up the theatre's lot the day after each show), when he was 14 in 1964, to the theatre's manager, when he was 21 in 1971. Here are some of his words:

On Being A Lot Boy

For the most part, lot boy was a lonely job. I would get there early in the morning, and about the only people I would see would be the occasional delivery person. Of course, the thrilling part came in the finds. People threw a lot more out than just trash. There was always money to find. I'm not saying I got rich, but a quarter here, a dime there, adds up. It was rare but not unusual to hit paydirt, with dollar bills. Then, of course, there was the unopened bottles of beer! I guess it was a good thing that, at age 14, that stuff tasted terrible to me and I had no use for it. But, as they say, one man's trash is another man's treasure. So I would save it for the snack bar guys. The term we used for this was to sink 'em. In the snack bar, we had a machine that made crushed ice. The bin that held the ice was

about two feet by two feet by two feet. I would take the unopened (beer) bottles and push them down to the bottom of the ice. I don't know what happened to them after that.

On Being A Soda Dispenser

Just before the intermission between shows I would put on a stiff white jacket and would stand behind the soda machine and pour Coke, orange, and Sprite through the entire intermission. It was neat the way it (the soda operation) was set up. The top of the machine consisted of a plastic cover that had rows of holes to hold the cups. I had an ice bucket next to me that I would use to scoop the ice into the cup. I'd then place the cup into the holder and fill it with soda from a hand-held nozzle dispenser. My trick was to always have soda ready so the people could just grab and run. Our goal was to get as many people through the snack-bar as we could before the next feature started, so all efforts were directed to having the food and soda ready to grab and run. But the real expertise of this job came from knowing when to slow down the pour. Of course I did not want to end the intermission with a rack full of unsold sodas, nor did I want anyone to wait for their drink. It took a lot of observation and mental energy on my part.

On The Fringe Benefits

Without a doubt, the greatest fringe benefit was the popcorn! At the drive-in we had this gigantic popcorn machine. The rule was that we could eat all the popcorn we wanted; we just couldn't use the popcorn containers! That was how inventory was done. There was always popcorn, day and night. In the morning, when I went to pick up the lot, I would grab a couple of handfuls, because we stored the leftovers right in the machine. But, at night time, there was nothing like freshly popped movie popcorn. I don't know how it is done today, but then we used to use coconut oil and this special yellow popcorn salt. Every night fresh popcorn was made, and right above the popcorn machine was a fan that would take the smell out into the theatre lot. It wasn't until I was manager myself that I learned the truth about theatres. As I learned, we were really in the popcorn business and we only showed movies to increase those sales!

On The Projectionist Missing A "Change Over" (the switching from one reel to another during the movie)

Of course, the manager would come into the booth to find out what happened, or if there was a serious problem. But when he realized that the projectionist had just missed the change over, he would just give a particular look and a sigh, and walk back out. Later, when I became the manager, I found it wasn't that difficult to learn that look and sigh combination. And I believe it worked better than any other admonishment.

The Kittery-York Drive-In opened on Thursday August 21, 1952, and closed on Monday, September 5, 1983. On opening night there was free popcorn. On closing night the show itself - in "appreciation" to the patrons who had supported the Drive-In over 30 seasons - was free. It was a nice way to say goodbye. The drive-in's former site is now buried beneath the rubble of the Kittery Outlet Malls on Route 1.

Ad, *The Portsmouth Herald*, July 7, 1955. Largely forgotten now, Mickey Spillane wrote some classic detective stories in his day. KISS ME DEADLY was one of his best. Nor did the movie adaptation disappoint. In his MOVIE & VIDEO GUIDE, Leonard Maltin described the movie as "years ahead of its time, and one of (director Robert) Aldrich's best films."

FORT KENT DRIVE-IN
FORT KENT

Photo, 1953. Courtesy of Marilyn Harvey, Fort Kent. The Fort Kent was opened by veteran theatre proprietor Charlie Brooks in the early 1950s. No one, though, seems to recall exactly when in the early 1950s. Area native Norman "Shorty" Long, 76, has the best recall, and he goes with 1952. I'll go with Shorty, who worked at both the Fort Kent and Presque Isle drive-ins for a solid dozen years in the fifties and sixties. "Back when I was young and foolish," he laughs.

Drive-Ins

Letterhead, circa 1970. Courtesy of Marilyn Harvey, Fort Kent. Frederick "Dick" Harvey and his wife Marilyn bought the drive-in from Charlie Brooks in 1969, ran it for a few years, then sold to one Clarence Levesque, who ran it until its closing in 1986. I asked Marilyn how she would characterize her drive-in years. Her reply: "It was quite a bit of work. And it tied us down. But it was fun. The people - the customers - made it fun."

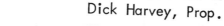

FORT KENT DRIVE-IN THEATRE

Dick Harvey, Prop.

P. O. Box 1
FORT KENT, MAINE 04743
Phone (207) 994-5800

"I remember the priest used to say in the pulpit that people shouldn't go to the drive-in as it was a passion pit," recalls 57-year old Fort Kent native Kenneth Michaud. Kenneth, now Fort Kent's Chief of Police, remembers that he went anyway. And sometimes, he laughingly admits, he and his teenage comrades would make their way in via an auto trunk. "We didn't have the money to pay," he explains.

Another Fort Kent native who well recalls teenage days at the drive-in is 43-year old Norma Voisine. She especially remembers the "all-nighters." The dusk-to-dawn extravaganzas. "That's the only time our parents would let us stay out late," she laughs. Norma's husband Richard, 50, however, has the most drive-in memories. He vividly recalls his all-time favorite Fort Kent Drive-In movie. It's THE NIGHT OF THE LIVING DEAD. "It was a horror movie. All about zombies. They'd come out of graves and chew up people. If you got scratched by one (of the zombies), then you would turn into a zombie. I really liked that movie," Richard sums up.

Richard also recalls his entrepreneurial days at the drive-in. "When I was in grammar school we'd (my friends and I) go to the drive-in and wash windshields. On a by-donation basis. We'd bring a bottle of Windex and a handful of paper towels and go for it." But Richard didn't stop there. "We'd also sell hazelnuts," he continues, "during the hazelnut season in August. We'd peel 'em during the week and sell 'em by the glassful before the show on weekends."

The Fort Kent Drive-In fell victim to the usual drive-in party poopers: vcrs, cable tv, etc. It closed in late July, 1986. Most of its former site, on Route 16 south of town, is now occupied by the Fish River Campgrounds.

105

PRESQUE ISLE DRIVE-IN PRESQUE ISLE

When they purchased the 17-year old - it had opened on May 8, l953 - Presque Isle Drive-In in 1970, the Bernard brothers probably knew that, for the most part, drive-ins had already seen their glory days. But the brothers, Richard (then 33), Reg (then 31), and Mike (the "baby" at 23), didn't much care. "Reg and I," details Mike, "had worked at the Boundary Line in Fort Fairfield. And we kind of got to like the business. It got in our blood. Maybe it was the novelty of it. It was," concludes Mike, "unlike any other business we'd ever worked in."

Mike's highlight in the years his brothers and he owned the drive-in was one shared with other theatre owners and employees I spoke with. It was the dusk-to-dawn shows: "We had an hour of cartoons followed by four full-length features. We'd do it three times a year, the night of the three holidays. We used to fill up with those. We really did run all night, too," stresses Mike. "In fact," and he chuckles some, "one time it was getting light and we still had an hours worth of the last film." Did the

brothers show that last hour? You bet they did. Mike also chuckles as he recalls another story. "I remember one time we had a thick fog come in. That was unusual, too, because Presque Isle is not near the ocean. It came in so quick that within ten minutes you couldn't see anything. We had an old crank telephone system and the projectionist rang us up and said 'There's something wrong. I can't see the picture on the screen.' We said 'Just keep running: they'll (the patrons) listen to the sound and follow the movie that way.' Then it - the fog - blew out as

Ad, Presque Isle *Star-Herald*, September 24, 1953. On the drive-in's former site there is now a Kingdom Hall of Jehovah's Witnesses.

Drive-Ins

quickly as it had come in and we could see the picture on the screen again."

The end for Mike, Reg, and Rich - and the drive-in - came in 1980. Two factors played a role in their decision to close. First was the addition of indoor screens to the area. "That really hurt," recalls Mike. As Rich explains: "People would say 'Why go to the drive-in when we can go to the air-conditioned Presque Isle Cinema (opened in 1969 and twinned in 1979)?" The second factor was more dramatic. "Our problem was our screen," Mike remembers all too well. "It wasn't boxed in (as with most other drive-ins), which would have helped with bad weather. And it would suffer from dry rot and wind damage. The insurance company," continues Mike, "covered repairs a time or two, but then they cancelled our policy. When it (screen damage) happened again we decided that repairing it wasn't worth it." The Presque Isle Drive-In's last show was August 29,1980. On the theatre's former site, on Route 1, South/the Houlton Road, there is now a Jehovah's Witnesses Kingdom Hall.

P.S. Drive-ins must have really been in Rich's blood. He later went on to own and operate the St. Croix Drive-In in Baring. (See page 120.)

PRIDES CORNER DRIVE-IN PRIDES CORNER (WESTBROOK)

The chances are very good that Herb Tevanian has owned and operated a drive-in - the *same* drive-in - longer than any other person in America. Or the world, for that matter. After all, 50 years is a long time. Herb, along with brothers Avadis ("Avie") and John, opened Prides Corner on May 13, 1953. Avadis' first wife's family owned several drive-ins in Massachusetts and that gave the brothers the thought of opening an outdoor movie theatre of their own.

An interviewee who well recalls at least some of the theatre's 50 years is 63-year old Ann (Hebert) Ridge, who frequented Prides Corner in the early l950s. "We - my friends and I - would go as two or three couples. That way," she chuckles, "if you weren't crazy about the guy you were with you didn't have to pay much attention to him." Really chuckling now, Ann thinks back again: "I remember this one guy - and my mother thought he was a 'nice boy' because he came from a 'nice family' - man, oh man, did I have to be rude to him, to keep him from taking advantage of the private situation." By "private situation," Ann meant the privacy afforded by being in a car. "As a teenager in those days," she reflects, "it (the drive-in) was the first time where others weren't involved in your privacy."

Another "rememberer" is Dale Rand. Dale, who hails from Portland and who's 57, has a double set of memories. The first set is from the 1960s when he and his-wife-to-be, Anne, went to the drive-in during their courting days. The second set is far more recent. "This past summer," he smiles, "Anne and I took our daughter Alicia, 13, to Prides Corner. We wanted her to have the chance to really enjoy it - the drive-in - like we had. She ended up loving all of it. She liked going to the concession stand and getting all the food and relaxing in the car." And, Dale adds,"We brought our dog Jack along, too. He loved it. He got fed all kinds of food."

Back to Herb, though. In talking with him one could easily get the notion that he's far from enthralled to have been in the drive-in business all these years. Asked for his favorite moment in his 50 years of summer nights he replies "It's hard to say. It's not too exciting. It's kind of a drag." But get him talking for awhile and Herb's deep affection for what he does begins to show through. "I like the people," he'll say. "I like the long days and the variety of each day. You're outdoors in the fresh air. It's not really," he sums up, "a bad job at all."

P.S. Avadis Tevanian died in 1988. For more on John Tevanian please see page 127.

Photo, 1953. Courtesy of John Tevanian, Portland. The screen you see here lasted until early 2001. Then it fell prey to a windstorm. Herb, daunted not the least, had a new model constructed in place of the old. The drive-in re-opened the last week of July, 2001.

Drive-Ins

Photo, 1953. Courtesy of John Tevanian, Portland. A favorite "ozoner" slogan was "See The Stars Under The Stars." Just as true, especially in this wonderful photo, is "See The Cars Under The Stars."

CORNISH DRIVE-IN
CORNISH

The Cornish Drive-In was part of Russell Martin's outdoor theatre "empire." (For Russell's story please see page 63.). The theatre opened in June 1953 with a showing of TITANIC. Not the 1997 opus, of course, but the 1953 version, starring Barbara Stanwyck, Clifton Webb, and Robert Wagner.

Martin ran the Cornish Drive-In until he sold it to then-24 year old Kezar Falls/South Hiram native Don Cross in 1960. "I had worked for him (Russell) in 1954 at the drive-in," explains Don, "and when I came out of the service in 1959 I went to see him." Russell, however, surprised Don by suggesting that he (Don) not only work at the drive-in but own it as well. The two did some figuring and, sure enough, Don ended up becoming proprietor. "I think I paid just about $10,000 in total," he thinks back. Then, continuing, Don laughs: "I got involved (with the theatre) because I didn't have a job and I said this will give me something to do in the summer and then I'll find something to do in the winter."

Don's "something to do in the summer" ended up lasting 20 years. When I asked him about highlights in those 20 years he replied that "There were more 'lowlights' than highlights."

That's because, relays Don, he bought the theatre at the time things were slowing down appreciably in the drive-in industry. By 1970 Don was just breaking even. Then along came a film distributor who suggested Don show X-rated films. "I was dubious," recalls Don. "This is a small town." But he decided to try it. "Well," he laughs, "I sold more tickets than anytime in the previous ten years. It was mostly the older generation. I used to say," Don laughs again, "it was the 'remembers' rather than the 'doers' who went to X-rated shows."

By 1980 Don decided he'd had enough of being a drive-in owner/operator. "Too many lean years," he puts it. He sold the theatre to Pembroke, New Hampshire native Howard Saturley. Saturley kept things going another three years. His biggest complaint: having to drive to Portland to get his movies. "It got to be a hassle after a while," he says. And with good reason. In addition, it was difficult to get *good* movies. "They (the distributors) told us what we could have," Howard laments. "We didn't have any choice on the films." Howard closed the drive-in in 1983. Its old site, on Route 25 between Cornish and Standish, is now occupied by a self-storage facility.

Drive-Ins

Cornish
Drive-In Theatre
Route 25, Cornish, Maine
Show Starts at Dusk
Admission 50c   Children Free

- - - - - - - - -

Program
Week of June 20, 1954

- - - - - - - - -

Cover and inside of Coming Attractions flyer, June 1954. You have to especially appreciate Milt Henry's "Any Car/Any Color = $39.95 and Up." Nowadays try getting even a fender painted for $39.95.

CORNISH DRIVE-IN THEATRE

Sunday thru Friday, feature plays first.   Saturday only, feature plays last.
Current Attractions advertised daily in Portland Press-Herald

Sun.-Mon.—June 20-21

Elsbeth Sigmund
Henrick Gretler   **'Heidi'**

'White Mane'   Color

● Monday is Jackpot Night

Tues.-Wed.-Thurs.—June 22-23-24

Marjorie Main
Percy Kilbride   **'Ma & Pa Kettle Back Home'**
Edward Arnold
Susan Morrow   **'Man of Conflict'**

Fri.-Sat.—June 25-26

Wanda Hendrix
Van Heflin   **'Golden Mask'**   Color
Rock Hudson
Donna Reed   **'Gun Fury'**   Technicolor

SKOWHEGAN DRIVE-IN THEATRE

WATERVILLE RD.   SKOWHEGAN, ME.

MON. and TUES. ☞ 'ENCYCLOPEDIA NITES'

SUNDAY & MONDAY   JULY 25 - 26

Esther WILLIAMS ★ Fernando LAMAS Technicolor

DANGEROUS WHEN WET

— AND —

THE BOWERY BOYS

LOOSE IN LONDON

TUES. - WED. - THUR.   JULY 27 thru 29

Barbara Stanwyck ★ Barry Sullivan

JEOPARDY

— PLUS —

Rhonda FLEMING ★ Gene BARRY

THOSE REDHEADS FROM SEATTLE

FRIDAY & SATURDAY   JULY 30 - 31

AUDIE MURPHY ★ LORI NELSON

TUMBLEWEED

— AND —

JOAN LESLIE ★ FORREST TUCKER

FLIGHT NURSE

Poster from the theatre's inaugural year, 1953. The "Encyclopedia Nites" are gone, but the drive-in, located on Route 201 south, is still going strong. You can thank Doug Corson - who will tell you how much he enjoys what he does, "especially the people I've had a chance to meet!" - for that.

Drive-Ins

SKOWHEGAN DRIVE-IN
SKOWHEGAN

"The gates will open at 7 P.M. with the show starting at dusk. The children's playground with it's (sic) merry-go-round, swings, chutes, will be open for the children's enjoyment before the show starts. Also the new and modern Snack Bar where one may purchase refreshments, will be open." So read the *Waterville Morning Sentinel* the morning of June 27, 1953, heralding the opening of the Skowhegan Drive-In. Added the *Sentinel*: "The finest in projection equipment insures a clear and brilliant picture on the giant 'Framed by the Stars' screen."

Doug Corson well recalls the drive-in's early years. He laughs as he relays how people would pay, even on the most crowded of evenings, just to be able to motor in and park, hoping to be able to pick up sound from other people's speakers. "We were definitely filled to capacity in those days," he beams. "Those days," for Doug, were the mid and late fifties. Doug started working at the drive-in in 1956, while still a student at Skowhegan High. He's been there every summer since, a model of longevity exceeded only by Prides Corner's Herb Tevanian. He's owned the theatre since 1985, sort of as a one-man band. Doug is the theatre's projectionist, booking agent, concession stand manager, and all-around jack-of-all-drive-in trades.

A person who definitely appreciates Doug's efforts is 32-year old Augusta-ite Stephanie Grenier. She fairly radiates as she tells of going to the drive-in with her husband Sam and their friends and their combined menage of kids, aged six to ten. "It was a nice night and the place was packed," says Stephanie. "We finally got in and we parked toward the back. Then we broke out the lawn chairs, blankets, stuff for the kids, and lots of food. We put the kids together in and around one car, the adults in and around the other. Being outdoors and not confined to a seat made it hard for us to sit in one spot and quietly watch the movie," admits Stephanie. But that was no problem. "The atmosphere made it more of a social event. We were having such a good time we really didn't pay much attention to the movie. It was fun!"

JAY HILL DRIVE-IN
JAY

For Bill Lee, who would drive to the Jay Hill from Weld, the drive-in was "something to do." For Casey and Charlie Young, who owned it, the drive-in was "always something to do." Therein lies the difference between being a patron of the arts and being the overseer, owner, and operator of them.

"Terrible" is how Casey Young, who was co-proprietor of the drive-in with her husband Charlie from 1964 on, characterizes their years at the Jay Hill. "You had to be there every night all summer long," says she, going on to mention that it was "just hard work." Casey and Charlie's daughter Kathy seconds that emotion, calling the family's drive-in years "a nightmare." Kathy does chuckle, though, when she recalls her father's green paint trick. As with just about every drive-in, kids would sneak into the theatre. At the Jay Hill they would make their way in via a hole under the fence. Charlie would often paint the bottom of the fence green just before showtime, so he could tell who snuck in. Did he then oust them from the drive-in? "No, he just laughed," smiles Kathy. "He felt the joke was on them."

Kathy's sister Kristi appears more upbeat when she looks back. "I remember," she says, "how exciting it was to arrive for the show and see how many cars would be lined up to get in. They (the customers) all had their favorite space. They'd park in the same place every week." Another Kristi memory is of the projector: "Sometimes, about once a month, the projector would get so hot it would melt the film. Then you'd have to take the film out and splice it together. All the people would honk their horns to try to speed things up."

Another event in the life of the theatre that brings smiles - more or less - to the family's faces is the locally infamous Ordinance #26. In the early 1970s, in an attempt to bolster sagging attendance, Charlie began to run X-rated films. It didn't set well with some of the key townspeople. The result was an ordinance, passed in March 1972, that prohibited "the operation of an outdoor motion picture theatre unless said theatre is suitably screened to prevent the projected picture or projection light from being visible from any public way or public place." To remain in business the Youngs had to erect a 45-foot high wall along Route 4.

The Jay Hill Drive-In, which had opened in July of 1953, closed in 1975, a victim of declining patronage and vandalism. Its former site, on Route 4 between Jay and North Jay/Wilton, is today occupied by an open field.

Drive-Ins

Coming Attractions flyer, July 1965. The Jay Hill did no newspaper advertising. These flyers, mailed to all local residents, were the theatre's way of announcing what was playing.

Photo, 1954. Courtesy of Mary Grant, Belfast. That's Mary and John's 1939 Ford closest to the screen. "Wish I still had it," she noted on the back of the photo.

BELFAST DRIVE-IN
BELFAST

By 1953, when the drive-in movie boom was still on the upswing, Maine had over two dozen drive-ins in operation. Graphic Theatres, Inc., a Boston-based theatre chain, decided one more was in order. The Belfast Drive-in was the result. Grand opening was August 8th. Ads touted all the features that drive-ins offered: "Come as you are", "Enjoy The Movies in The Comfort Of Your Car!", and that great clincher with so many young parents, "No baby sitters!" On the screen was Mitzi Gaynor in THE I DON'T CARE GIRL, and Ann Blyth and Robert Mitchum in ONE MILLION TO ZERO.

The crowds came. *The Belfast Republican* reported a capacity turnout, noting "Belfast's newest entertainment center offers the latest in drive-in facilities."

In a 1992 interview with the late John Grant of Belfast he recalled the drive-in's glory days. John had managed the theatre from 1955 on. His fondest memory was the time he masterminded a lobster night in the early 1960s. For 75¢ a patron could view the movies; for but a $1.00 more he or she could also enjoy a lobster supper. John beamed as he recalled having to repeatedly send down to Drinkwater's Lobster Pound on Northport Avenue to

Drive-Ins

replenish his supply.

John's widow Mary, in a February 2001 interview, recalled something less fun. "I remember it (the theatre) flooded every time it rained. The concession stand/projection booth. Oh, dear, we'd walk around in water with all that equipment there. Looking back, it was pretty dangerous. It was especially bad in the spring, but any rainstorm would do it. We were actually in a swamp. The concession stand kept sinking lower and lower. The worst time," and here Mary allows herself a chuckle, "was when this little brook that flowed behind where the cars would park overflowed. It turned out there were beavers there and they'd built a dam. The state game wardens had to come and blow up the dam."

What are you almost guaranteed to find in swampy turf? Yep, mosquitos. And that's what 52-year old Belfast-native Dixie Sanders recalls the most about the drive-in. "If it was hot you wanted to roll your windows down, but the mosquitos liked to come in and nibble." Still, though, Dixie has fond memories of the theatre. "There weren't a lot of things to do and so you went to the drive-in. It wasn't expensive and it was fun."

The fun waned, per John, from about 1960 on. Television and video rentals hurt. So did the negativism generated by drive-ins' "passion pit" image. John experimented with special nights, X-rated films, other draws. Nothing made much of a difference. By the early 1980s business was lean. By the mid-1980s it was worse. On August 24, 1986 John showed RAMBO and ABOUT LAST NIGHT and then closed. For good. Today the theatre's old site, just to the left of Reny's Plaza on Route 3/the Augusta Road, is an empty (and probably still swampy) field.

Photo, February 1993. For many years after the theatre's closing its signboard remained up and relatively intact. Even it, however, is now gone.

117

BOUNDARY LINE DRIVE IN THEATRE

Fort Fairfield
One show nightly starting
at 7:30 p. m.

THU., OCT. 21
"Ruby Gentry"
starring
Charlton Heston
Jennifer Jones
Cartoon   Shorts

FRI., OCT. 22
"Destination Gobi"
(Technicolor)
with
Richard Widmark
Don Taylor
Cartoon   Shorts

SAT., OCT. 23
"Powder River"
(Technicolor)
starring
Rory Calhoun Corrin Calvet
also
"My Pal Gus"
Richard Widmark
Joanne Dru

SUN., OCT. 24
"Monkey Business"
starring
Marilyn Monroe
Cartoon   Shorts

MON. thru FRI.
OCT. 25 thru 29
Closed

SAT., OCT. 30
"Treasure of the Golden Condor"
(Technicolor)
Cornel Wilde
Constance Smith
also

Ad, *Fort Fairfield Review*, October 1954. Courtesy of Lois Shelp, Fort Fairfield. Business boomed in those early days. "For some movies," fondly recalls Lois Shelp, "there'd be a line of cars down the road a mile or so."

BOUNDARY LINE DRIVE-IN FORT FAIRFIELD

When it came to the Boundary Line Drive-In the Dean family was somewhat akin to president Grover Cleveland: they were in office, then out of office, then back in office. Let's begin with Dean proprietorship number one. That was Stinson Dean. "My father Stinson was a potato farmer," recalls Lois (Dean) Shelp, 65, Stinson's daughter, "who decided one day that he wanted to do something in addition to farming." Lois remembers her dad took a trip to Houlton, talked to the proprietor of the Borderland Drive-in, and returned home ready to go.

The Boundary Line - so named because it was very near the New Brunswick border - opened in July of 1954. It was a success from the start.

Drive-Ins

Of course, as Lois puts it so well, "That's (the fifties) when everybody went to the drive-in, and the theatre used to fill up most of the time. For some movies there'd be a line of cars down the road a mile or so." A "highlight" of those years was "the streaker." Lois, who worked at the theatre as ticket-taker and bookkeeper at the time, laughs as she recalls that one night, during a dusk-to-dawn extravaganza in the late sixties, a streaker suddenly appeared out of nowhere, ran around the screen a couple of times, and then disappeared as quickly as he'd arrived. "We never did catch him," chuckles Lois.

Stinson, with considerable help from his wife Hazel as well as Lois, ran the Boundary Line until 1970. He then leased it to Donald Dorsey (see page 129). "I think at that time they (her dad and mom) had reached a point where they were tired of it (the theatre)," says Lois. "They wanted to have more free time."

Dorsey ran the theatre four years and then wanted out. So Lois stepped in. "I kind of wanted to have a business of my own," she explains, "and it was there and was something I really knew about." The only problem was that, by the mid-1970s, drive-ins were no longer thriving. When asked about her years as proprietor, Lois answers "It was alright." But that's about it. Nevertheless, Lois ran the operation seven years until she, too, had had it. She sold to a couple named Jim and Karen Everitt. They eked a few more seasons out of the theatre before closing it in September of 1984. The drive-in's former site, on the Boundary Line Road heading toward New Brunswick, is now an open field.

ST. CROIX VALLEY DRIVE-IN
BARING

"See The Stars Under The Stars" rang out the ads for the St. Croix Valley Drive-In when it opened the first week of July 1954, just in time for the big 4th of July weekend. The original owners were local businessmen Allie Nasson and K.J. "Doc" Thomas. Within a year they were joined by K.J.'s son, Kenneth Smith "Smitty" Thomas. "They wanted some young blood," jests the now 73-year old Smitty.

"It was a big deal when it opened," recounts Smitty. "I believe we had, at 80 feet wide by 58 feet tall, the second largest drive-in screen in Maine. Only the Portland's (screen) was bigger." Westerns and musicals were the favorites. So was the food. A lot of people, in fact, would come more to eat, both Smitty and his son, 42-year old Ken Thomas, recall proudly. Homemade French fries were the biggest seller, but the drive-in's hot dynamites - spicy meatball sandwiches made especially for the 4th of July - satisfied many a palate as well.

A memory from all those years ago that still gets Smitty laughing with vigor was his attempt to do away with the theatre's mosquito population. He sprayed the entire drive-in area with a solution that was 25% DDT. "We killed everything but the mosquitos," he smiles. "It didn't bother them at all."

Smitty became the theatre's sole proprietor in 1962, and both owned and operated it until 1976, when, tired of the pressure of running both the drive-in and a newer venture, the International Motel, he sold the theatre to then 39-year old Rich Bernard. Rich, a native of Caribou, was a teacher who had tired of teaching. The result was that, in conjunction with his two brothers, he'd bought the Braden Theatre and the Presque Isle Drive-In (q.v.), both in Presque Isle, in 1970.

Rich chuckles as he recalls his St. Croix Valley opening. He'd purchased the drive-in in late 1976, so the opening was in 1977. Come the grand evening - it was April, Rich remembers - it was snowing hard. "Snowing to beat hell," as Rich so clearly phrases it. He was all set to call the whole thing off until he noticed that cars, lots of cars, were lining up for the show. "If

Drive-Ins

Ad, 1963. Many people came to the drive-in as much for the food as for the show.

they're crazy enough to watch a movie in this snowstorm, I'm crazy enough to show it," declared Rich. And he did.

All went relatively well at the drive-in until 1994. That's when Rich and his wife Lucille decided to focus on another theatre they owned, the State in downtown Calais. They put the St. Croix Valley up for sale. More accurately, they put the *land* on which the drive-in stood up for sale: whoever purchased the property had to agree not to use it as a drive-in. That was because Rich and Lucille didn't want a new owner to be competing with the State. Rich and Lucille did, however, keep the St. Croix Valley going until a buyer came along. That sad occurence happened just a year later, in 1995. The drive-in's last show was in September of that year. The theatre's old site in Baring, just southwest of Calais, is now occupied by a warehouse.

No drive-in was/is complete without a supply of fog passes. Here's one - greatly enlarged - from Oxford's all-time favorite drive-in.

NORWAY ❖ DRIVE-IN THEATRE

ROUTE 26 • OXFORD PLAINS • NORWAY, MAINE

FOG PASS

ADMIT ONE

SUBJECT TO CONDITIONS BELOW

Good Next Performance

This ticket is issued in lieu of refund for an interrupted Show due to inclement weather or mechanical failure and will be honored at the next scheduled performance.

PLEASE SURRENDER AT BOX OFFICE

Drive-Ins

NORWAY DRIVE-IN
OXFORD

"I was looking for a business to start. And both the indoor theatres in the area - in Norway and in South Paris - had closed. So a drive-in seemed a good opportunity." That's Lester Soule's reason for getting into the drive-in theatre business.

The Norway Drive-In opened September 1, 1954. Lester owned and operated it for a solid decade, before selling in 1963. His favorite memory from that drive-in decade is a good one. It was the day BEN HUR came to town. "We had a parade when (the movie) BEN HUR played. It was circa 1959. I'd seen the previews," continues Lester, "and I thought a parade might stir up some interest. We had a man dressed up in a toga and riding in a chariot, and a line of cars with signs playing up the movie. They drove down Main Street. It was a winner for us. Both the parade and the movie. BEN HUR was the most successful movie we ever had. The most receipts," Lester fondly recalls. "We filled up three nights in a row and that was something."

From 1963 to 1977 the drive-in saw a string of proprietors. Then Bob and Elinore Kingsley came along. "My father had theatre in his blood," states Bob and Elinore's daughter, Elaine (Kingsley) Rioux. "He had managed the drive-in for a number of years, liked what he saw, decided to buy it," continues Elaine. Elinore ran the snack bar while Bob handled everything else, including being the drive-in's goodwill ambassador. "He loved to stand outside the snack bar and visit with people," Elaine warmly remembers.

Elaine also fondly recalls a rather wonderful Norway Drive-In tradition. It seems a set of train tracks ran alongside Route 26 in front of the theatre's entrance. One evening the train's engineer tooted his whistle as he passed the drive-in. The theatre's ticket taker responded by flipping on the theatre's marquee lights. Both parties got a kick out of it, repeated it the next night... and thus was born a custom that would be repeated every summer evening until the end for the drive-in came in 1985. That was the year cable tv came to the area. Business nosedived. "It was a sad thing to watch," says Elaine and her husband Richard, remembering back to the decision to shut the theatre - and its marquee lights - down. On the theatre's old site, just south of Oxford True Value, there is now not much of anything. The old snack bar still stands, but that's about it.

KATAHDIN DRIVE-IN
MATTAWAMKEAG

"It was the fault of the men (that the Katahdin Drive-In closed down in 1984). They should have taken all the tvs to the dump." So states almost-lifetime Mattawamkeag resident Keith "Red" Hale, 72, continuing, "It was the tvs that killed it (the drive-in.). We had an indoor theatre, too. The Cameo. And it (tv) did that one in, too." Although his opinion could certainly be classified as sexist, Red's probably not far from right. The Katahdin's mosquito

"Welcome" sign, Route 157, July 2001. Mattawamkeag is today but a shadow of its old-time self. Gone is the Katahdin. Gone is the Cameo. And gone is any semblance of a real downtown.

population, however, didn't help either. "There was a river right across the road. That caused a lot of mosquitos," admits 59-year old Winn native Clifford Faulkner. "They (theatre management) used to run a rig and spray before the show," Clifford adds, "but it only helped some."

What else do people recall about the Katahdin Drive-In? An assortment of things. Carlton Norris, 59, remembers the popcorn. "I don't know what it was," he says, "but it was good. It only cost a quarter and you'd get a bag that was big. Real big." Violet Pettengill recalls that the theatre was well kept in the beginning. "Then it started to deteriorate. It began to look like it needed paint." Clifford Faulkner, back again, fondly recalls the buck-a-car nights. "We'd all pile in a car and raise a little hell. We were young fellows then."

The Katahdin Drive-in opened on May 13, 1955 and closed on August 26, 1984. Its former site, four miles from Mattawamkeag on Route 157, has been largely reclaimed by nature. There are shrubs. There are trees. And there are mosquitos.

Drive-Ins

MIDWAY DRIVE-IN DETROIT

MIDWAY *Drive-In* BETWEEN NEWPORT AND PITTSFIELD MAINE'S NEWEST AND FINEST

GIANT SCREEN

Now Showing
"THIS PROPERTY IS CONDEMNED"
Natalie Wood
Robert Bedford
plus
"SLENDER THREAD"
Sidney Poitier
Anne Bancroft
Fri. & Sun. Main Feature
Showing at 7:30

June 1955 was a banner month for the Newport/Pittsfield area. The largest Tastee Freeze in the State of Maine opened in Newport. The president of the United States, Dwight D. Eisenhower, visited Pittsfield. And the Midway Drive-In Theatre sprang into operation midway between the two, in Detroit.

The Grand Opening of the drive-in was Thursday, June 16th. Admission was 50¢ for adults. "Kiddies" were free. On the screen - "one of Maine's largest and finest Cinemascope screens," lauded *The Pittsfield Advertiser* - was Alfred Hitchcock's REAR WINDOW, starring Grace Kelly and James Stewart, and George Montgomery in THE LONE GUN.

The Midway's stated goal was "to give the surrounding communities the best in shows, food, and service." No one could dispute the theatre's success in achieving that goal at first. Rocky Connors of Pittsfield remembers taking his whole family to the drive-in on many an occasion. His kids liked the playground. He liked the fact that the grounds were kept clean and well-maintained. Newport native Don Hallenbeck was a kid when he went to the Midway. He, too, recalls the playground (especially, as he puts it, "the obligatory swing set"), and that it was very well kept. In the mid-1970s, however, the Midway became known as the "Ill-Repute Theatre," with a steady stream of x-rated films. That got to a lot of folks in Detroit. First selectman Joe Schissler recalls "We had people coming in and complaining." Finally, no one recollects exactly when, the town passed an anti-obscenity ordinance, geared to get the Midway to close down or mend its "evil" ways.

Between pressure from the town and competition from tv and videos, the Midway wound down. It finally closed after the 1985 season. By then, states Joe Schissler, "There was absolutely no financial return."

Part of the theatre yet stands: the former concession stand/projection building. You can see it, looking rather forlorn, on the right about 2.2 miles east of Pittsfield on Routes 11 and 100.

GREENLAND DRIVE-IN
EAST MACHIAS

At the former Greenland Motel you could rent a room and/or view a movie. That's because the Greenland was a motel and drive-in all in one. It was constructed in early 1956 by William Green, Sr., a Latham, New York native who'd hunted in the Machias area for years.

Green's first show was June 19, 1956. Ads in *The Machias Valley News Observer* read "Enjoy the Movies under the Stars." Motel patrons, however, could enjoy the movies under the comfort of their roof. Each room included a speaker and an almost wall-to-wall picture window through which the theatre's large screen could clearly be seen.

Most of the theatre's viewers were, of course, folks sitting in their car or a lawn chair. Just like a regular drive-in. Sixty-seven year old Whiting native Christine Small was one of those folks. "You'd drive up and hopefully you'd find a speaker that worked," she laughs.

Christine also recalls the social aspect of the drive-in: "You could go and you could have friends in the next car. Sometimes the dads would sit in one car with the sons and the moms would sit in the other with the daughters."

The Greenland eventually fell prey to the dwindling economics that plagued most drive-ins. In February 1970 the theatre's screen blew down. William Green took that as an omen: he did not re-open.

The Greenland Motel is now the Maineland Motel, with Harold Prescott and his wife Barbara the owners and operators. I asked Harold if people still come by and reminisce. "Oh, yeah," he replied. "They'll say 'We used to come here.' Some people will say 'This can't be the place: there isn't anything out there.'"

But it is the place. And what's out there is memories. Fourteen years of them.

Ad, *The Coastal Courier*, July 28, 1963. Courtesy of Christine Small, East Machias. There has been only one drive-in theatre in Maine that could run this ad for a combination theatre/motel... the Greenland.

Drive-Ins

BRIDGTON DRIVE-IN BRIDGTON

Maine's drive-in movie mogul, Russell Martin (see write-ups for Naples, Sanford, and Cornish drive-ins), opened his fourth and last outdoor theatre in Bridgton in 1957. And he opened with a bang: on the screen for his Grand Opening, Friday June 14th, was THE GIRL CAN'T HELP IT, the rock 'n roll movie that starred Jayne Mansfield and Tom Ewell, with cameo appearances by Fats Domino, Little Richard (who sang the title track), the Platters, the Treniers, others. The theatre featured a 50' x 80' screen and was reportedly the first theatre in Maine to have a screen built exclusively for CinemaScope. Capacity was 350 cars. What Russell's daughter, Sharon (Martin) Remick, best recalls, though, is the theatre's concession stand. "The concession stand had large doors that opened up," says Sharon, "so that patrons could actually sit at little tables off to one side of the stand and look out to see the screen."

Sharon also recalls helping her parents put up cardboard posters in shops and stores in the area. She liked to help because, to make things fun, her mother or father would stop for ice cream along the way. "I especially recall there was a place in Hiram Falls," Sharon still beams. "It was an old-fashioned ice cream stand with all homemade ice cream. I'd always have a chocolate cone. It was great."

Forty-five years and two owners later the Bridgton Drive-In is still packing them in. Portland native John Tevanian (himself a Maine drive-in titan!), then 44, purchased the drive-in in 1971. He's been running it - with considerable assistance from his son, also named John - ever since. Not only has the duo kept the theatre alive and well, the almost unthinkable happened in the year 2000. The Tevanians expanded! They added a second screen. The theatre was, in the parlance of the trade, "twinned." "It was something we did in order to survive," states John the younger. "To attract more people during the (relatively) few weeks that make up the summer." When I inquired of John how it felt the day the second screen was opened to the world, on July 7, 2000, he reflected a bit and then answered, "It was a moment of accomplishment."

GRAND OPENING
BRIDGTON DRIVE-IN
Route 302   Bridgton-Naples Road
BOX OFFICE OPENS at 7 — SHOW STARTS at DUSK
FEATURE PLAYS FIRST EVERY NIGHT EXCEPT SATURDAY

Ad, *The Bridgton News*, June 13, 1957. The Bridgton Drive-In opened with a bang. Rock 'n roll greats Fats Domino, Little Richard, and the Platters all came to town! Via film, of course.

ESCOURT DRIVE-IN
ESCOURT STATION

Escourt Station almost makes Fort Kent seem like Palm Beach. Look at a Maine map and you'll see what I mean. And there are only two ways to reach it from the rest of the United States: via Quebec or via private lumber company roads. It just kind of hangs up there all by itself, with a population of about 55. So why would anyone want to build a drive-in there? Amelia Daigle, now 88, has the answer.

"We built it in 1958. My husband (Leo Daigle, 1910-1994) and me. He had the dealership for Buick and Chevrolet in Fort Kent. There was a man who would come to Fort Kent to pick up the mail for Escourt Station. He was always after my husband: 'Why don't you build something. An outdoor theatre or something to bring people to Escourt Station?' So my husband said to me, 'Can you take over the dealership and I'll build the theatre?' And he did. He did it all himself. He bulldozed the field, built the screen, did it all. He started in May and our first show was August 12th (1958). The people came from Quebec. (Ed. note: it was illegal to operate a drive-in theatre in the Province of Quebec at the time.). It was packed full. A lot of people didn't know how to park,

Coming Attractions flyer, July 1968. Courtesy of Amelia Daigle, Fort Kent. The drive-in's movies were just about always in French as most all the theatre's business came from neighboring Quebec.

Drive-Ins

though. We had five or six men to show them how. Some people would still park backwards. We could fit 200 cars. A few more if needed. My husband was the projectionist. I ran the canteen. Our children helped, too... taking tickets, working in the canteen. It was real family.

At first we were open four nights: Thursday, Friday, Saturday, Sunday. But we learned it was better if we were just open three nights: Friday, Saturday, Sunday. We opened the first week in May and closed two weeks after Labor Day.

We almost didn't open. There was a priest who ran a (regular indoor) theatre in nearby Escort, Quebec. He didn't want us to open. He was afraid it would hurt his business. He caused quite a squawk. But we got the help of the priest in Fort Kent and he said 'If it's (the drive-in) in the U.S.A. and it's legal, go ahead. There's nothing he can do to stop you.'

We sold the theatre because we were getting a little older and because it was difficult to get help. It (running the theatre) became too much bother. We sold it in 1983. A fellow bought it and then ran it for a few years. And then another (man) did, too. Finally it was torn down and there's a filling station there now. But the big screen still stands."

DORSEYLAND DRIVE-IN CARIBOU

Opened in August of 1962 by one Don Dorsey, the Dorseyland is usually recalled around town as the more "risque" of Caribou's two drive-ins. And for good reason: by 1965 the theatre was showing the likes of SINDERELLA AND THE GOLDEN BRA, and ROOM 43 ("Nothing Hidden!... Neither The Sin Nor The Shame!").

A man who recalls many Dorseyland years is Roland Cyr, Jr., 63, the theatre's projectionist from 1965 to 1970. "One evening I was closed up," he says with a chuckle. "The police chief stopped the show and took possession of the (x-rated) movie. It was okay with me: I got an evening off and got paid for it."

Another happening that Roland recalls was the locally-renowned Chain Saw Incident. "The theatre had a big wooden screen," he relates. "One winter somebody took a chain saw and cut down the screen's supports. The whole thing collapsed. We never did find out who it was that did it."

The Dorseyland changed proprietors and name in 1981-1982. It became the Hilltop Drive-In, remaining in operation until 1989. On its former site, on Route 84 East, there is now an ACAP (Aroostook County Action Program) facility.

SKYLITE DRIVE-IN MADAWASKA

The Skylite is Maine's newest drive-in. And it's a delight. "The thing we enjoy most about the drive-in," beams co-owner/co-operator Donna Pelletier, "are our customers. Especially the older generation. They come in with all kinds of (drive-in) stories that we love to listen to." Continues Donna: "Then there's the children who come for the first time. They are amazed with the big screen."

Photo, 1993. Courtesy of Donna Pelletier, Madawaska. Donna, right, and snack bar staff pose as part of the theatre's 20th anniversary celebration. The snack bar's biggest seller then: fried clams. The snack bar's biggest seller now: fried clams... with doughboys in hot pursuit.

What's especially rewarding about the Skylite is that it's such a family affair. Donna 38, and her husband Gary, 41, are the theatre's proprietors, but there's a trio of "co-proprietors" - Gary and Donna's offspring - on the job, too. Of course, the "familyness" of it all is not awfully surprising: the Skylite is just carrying on a drive-in tradition that goes back to the industry's very beginnings. In Gary and Donna's case the tradition goes back to Gary's grandfather, Raoul Chasse, who was involved with the nearby Madawaska Drive-In (see pages 95-96). Then came Rosaire and Lorraine (Chasse) Pelletier, Gary's folks. They opened the Skylite in 1973. In 1982 Gary and Donna took over the drive-in on the hill. "That was his - Gary's - life dream," beams Donna again, "to run the drive-in."

Waiting in the wings is the fourth generation. Jayme (17) helps Donna in the canteen. Austin (11) is enamored of the projector. Evan (10) is a one-person good-will ambassador. "He's our social bug," explains Donna. "He'll go to every car and talk to people."

Donna closed our November 2001 conversation with these words: "We're just one family trying to keep an American tradition alive." It sounds a mite trite... but not when you hear Donna say it.

Drive-Ins

Getting Ready For A New Season

Checking the speakers: Austin, Jayme, Evan and their grandfather, Rosaire, 1997

Shoveling out: Evan and Austin about a month before the theatre's opening, 1998. "Kids," Donna has noted on the back of the photo, "are excited."

Both photos courtesy of Donna Pelletier, Madawaska

Photos, left to right:
"Seperate Admission" (Actually, it should be "Separate.") sign, Bridgton Twin Drive-In (Note: no other active drive-in in Maine has to worry about more than one screen because no other active drive-in in Maine has more than one screen.); circa 1953 snack bar Coke sign, Prides Corner Drive-In; original 1953 marquee, Prides Corner Drive-In; original 1953 entrance sign, Showhegan Drive-In; sign on ticket booth, Skowhegan Drive-In.

STILL GOING STRONG AFTER ALL THESE YEARS

According to the United Drive-in Theatre Owners Association, there are approximately 435 drive-in theatres in operation on any given summer night across America. Five of them are located in Maine. They are: the Saco Drive-in (in operation in Saco since 1939); Prides Corner Drive-In (in operation in the Prides Corner section of Westbrook since 1953); Skowhegan

Drive-Ins

Photos, continued:
Ticket booth and screen, Skylite Drive-In; ticket booth "Closed" sign, Saco Drive-In; ticket booth, Skowhegan Drive-in; marquee, Skowhegan Drive-In; marquee, Saco Drive-In. All photos summer, 2001.

Drive-In (in operation in Skowhegan since 1953); Bridgton Drive-In (in operation in Bridgton since 1957; has been the Bridgton Twin Drive-In since July of 2000); Skylite Drive-In (in operation in Madawaska since 1973). Long may their show start at dusk.

R. HUBSCH

WERE FRIED CLAMS REALLY INVENTED IN MAINE?: THE FRIED CLAM STORY

The folks at Woodman's restaurant in Essex, Massachusetts claim that their eatery was the birthplace of the fried clam. That Woodman's founding father, Lawrence "Chubby" Woodman, accidentally discovered the technique while in Woodman's kitchen one day in July of 1916. It's a nice story and I'm sure that Mr. Woodman did "invent" the fried clam as far as he was concerned. The only problem: the fried clam had been around for at least a quarter of a century before Mr. Woodman made his discovery.

The chances are fair to good, in fact, that Maine was the birthplace of the fried clam. We know it's not likely to have been invented in Iowa. Or Kansas. Or North Dakota. No ocean = no clams. But Maine has ocean, and lots of it. And clams have long been a part of the Pine Tree State's gastronomical heritage. Here's what we know for sure.

Fried Clams

"Fried York Clams"

Dean Merchant, of Stratham, New Hampshire, has done *considerable* research in writing his forthcoming book, THE LORE OF THE FRIED CLAM. The earliest fried clam recipe he has been able to unearth goes back to 1889. In that year the ladies of the First Baptist Church, in Exeter, New Hampshire, gathered together a collection of "Valuable Recipes" and published them as a book entitled THE EXETER COOK BOOK. On page 16 is a recipe for Fried York Clams submitted by one Fred Prescott of York Beach, Maine. Here is that recipe.

> Fried York Clams - Roll three crackers very fine, beat one egg and add one pint of drained clams. Put in a very little milk if necessary. Fry in equal parts of pork fat and butter.

Did Fred Prescott invent the fried clam? Almost certainly not. Dean Merchant has found references to fried clams being a part of shore dinners in coastal Massachusetts earlier in the 1880s (and believes the same was true for Maine, too). But Mr. Prescott's pioneering recipe certainly helped to spread Maine's clam fame.

It would be another decade before our fried friends would work their way into the "media" of the day: the newspaper. And then, as might be expected, it was in the form of advertising. July 1899 ads in *The Bath Daily Times* and the *Lewiston Evening Journal* touted the fried clams at Merrymeeting Park, a large amusement complex located in Brunswick. For your viewing pleasure, *The Daily Times'* ad is reproduced on the following page. The *Evening Journal* ad was much the same, although not as visually attractive. It did, however, include prices. The table d'hote tariff for what was undoubtedly a

THE CASINO

Merrymeeting Park, Brunswick
SUNDAY MENUS. JULY 9

Regular Table d' Hote Dinner 75 cents - - - Shore Dinner 50 cents

Hours 12 to 3 and 6 to 8 o'clock

Dining Rooms open from 10 a. m. to 11 p. m - European Plan

Table 'd Hote
MENU

Olives

Lobstew Stew   Fish Chowder
Steamed Clams

Boiled Salmon with Peas
Pommes Parisenne
Cucumbers   Radishes

Plain Lobster with Lettuce

Fried Clams, Saratoga Chips

Roast Domestic Duck, Apple Sauce
Mashed Potatoes   Stewed Tomatoes

Strawberry Shortcake with
Whipped Cream

Vanilla or Chocolate Ice Cream
Assorted Cake

Crackers and Cheese
Coffee

Shore Dinner
MENU

Fish Chowder   Clam Chowder

Steamed Clams Drawn Butter
Cucumbers   Radishes

Plain Lobster with Lettuce

Fried Clams, Saratoga Chips

Ice Cream   Assorted Cake

Crackers and Cheese

Tea   Coffee

JAMES A. FULLER,
Proprietor and Manager of Casino and all Refreshment Pavilions on the Park Grounds.

Telephone Connection.

Ad, *The Bath Daily Times*, July 8, 1899. "Saratoga Chips" was an early name for potato chips, reflective of the fact that they were invented and first enjoyed in Saratoga Springs, New York.

Fried Clams

healthy portion of fried clams and Saratoga chips: 30¢.

The *Daily Eastern Argus - the* Portland paper of its time - saw its first mention (that I could find) of fried clams a year later. In its July 18, l900 issue there ran a large advertisement for Shaw's (yes, Shaw's) that featured fried clams in its delicatessen department (yes, its "deli" department). The ad offered for sale "Fried Scarboro Clams," stressing that they were "all HOT."

Two years later, in a booklet published by an organization known as the Woman's Relief Corps of Portland, there appeared an ad for the Riverton Casino, Portland, in which the Casino stated that they were "prepared at all times to serve Meals." The Casino further stated that its house specialties were steak and, you guessed it, fried clams. It is noteworthy that the Relief Corps' booklet also contained a page of recipes and that one of those recipes was for the batter in which to fry clams.

Other early Maine eateries that ballyhooed their fried clams included Cordes' Cafe, Portland (which advertised clams that were "rolled in Crumbs and done to a turn"); Boone's (which advertised "Try Our Fried Casco Bay Clams," and at the very same Portland waterfront location they yet occupy all these years later); West Gray's Gray Road Inn (which advertised fried clams in both crumbs and batter at 50¢ a small box; $1.00 a large one); the Earlcliff, located on the State Road (U.S. Route 1) in Scarborough; and Fournier's Cafe, located at 288 Main Street in Biddeford, which suggested that their Friday fried clam special really was something special.

Were fried clams invented in Maine? Maybe yes. Maybe no. In either case they've been pleasing Maine palates for a long, long time.

Some olden-day ads from places you may - or may not - remember. The Andy's ad is from 1947; The Clam Shell, Sim's, Ernie's, Chick-Land, and The Friends are all from 1950; The Fellsmore, 1951; Happy Jack, 1961; and Adrien's, 1965. I especially like Sim's Drive-In's "Snappy Girls For Snappy Curb Service."

A TRIBUTE TO A REPRESENTATIVE FEW

I suppose that, if one really wanted to work at it, one might be able to track down just about most every Maine eatery that's ever served up a batch of fried clam goodies. But that would necessitate a 700 or so-page book. And who wants a 700-page book? Instead, over the following eight pages, we've tracked down "life story" highlights for a representative few old-time Maine fried clam strongholds.

SIM'S DRIVE-IN

Open 12 Noon Til 2 A.M.

DELICIOUS LOBSTER ROLLS

- Fresh Crabmeat Rolls
- Pepper Steaks
- Fried Clams
- French Fried Potatoes
- Hamburgers
- Hot Dogs
- Cheeseburgers
- Frozen Custard

—Snappy Girls For Snappy Curb Service—

Mechanic Falls Rd.   Auburn   Dial 4-5011

Opening Friday, June 20 at 4 P.M.

ANDY'S

End of Carlton Bridge, Woolwich, formerly Toll-house Inn

Lobster Stew, Salads, Rolls, Etc. Fried Clams, French Fried Potatoes

Steaks, Chicken Chow Mein

Hot Dogs, Hamburgers, Sandwiches of all kinds.

Open Daily 10 A.M., to 2 A.M. Dancing Permitted from 8 P.M., to 12 P.M.

ANDREW B. HART, Prop.

Announcing Opening of

CHICK-LAND

Sunday, June 11

Specializing in Chicken-In-The-Basket, Steaks, Fried Clams.

Curb Service and Dining Room

Phone Bel. 739-W5,
Rt. 1 Northport, Maine

Postcard view, circa 1962.

ALCORN'S
HOULTON

Judy Hutchinson, 48, remembers Alcorn's as a place to which her family would sometimes go on a summer Sunday afternoon when she was nine or ten, in the early 1960s. She'd have a hamburger, French fries, and a shake. She did not partake of Alcorn's noted fried clams because, she thinks back, "My family ate a lot of seafood; burgers were more special."

Lynn York, 56, recalls Alcorn's as "a fry joint." What especially stands out for Lynn is that it was the first place where he ever witnessed zig zag-cut French fries. "I thought that was something unusual," he recounts.

Other Houltonites recall Alcorn's less for its food than its notoriety. Local hearsay has it that Sid Alcorn, Alcorn's proprietor, liked to hire attractive female help and then work with them perhaps closer than he should. Eventually, the hearsay unfolds, Sid's wife Eileen caught up to what was going on. The result: Sid skipped town. "In the middle of the night," as one source puts it.

Alcorn's opened in 1961 and closed when its namesake hit the road, circa 1966. Its distinctive five-sided structure still stands, on Route 2A, just south of the Houlton city limit. It is today a convenience store.

Fried Clams

ED'S GROVE
LYMAN

For over 30 years, from 1945 to 1976, Ed's Grove was *the* place to go for fried clams in Lyman, Waterboro, Hollis, Dayton, et al. As Waterboro native Chauncey Geery, 76, sums up: "Everybody knew of Ed's Grove. They had the best fried clams in the area. I think," he adds, "they had a secret recipe or something." Ed's was founded by Ed Berry. He then sold to Ed McGlaughlin, who, in turn, sold to Ed Wormwood. The three Eds. Ed number three, now 65, kept the fried clam tradition going. "Everybody said they were the best around," he recalls. Circa 1970, though, Ed went to repair a buckling floor and discovered his building had been badly burned at one point. Rather than attempt to fix what he thought was a losing proposition, Ed eventually tore the structure down, replacing it with the convenience store/eatery, R.B.'s Restaurant/3-D Energy Food Store, that's there today. Fried clams are still on the menu. "But they're not the same as ours were," Ed makes clear.

P.S. Ed Wormwood has kept Ed's Grove alive - sort of - by opening a discount store across Route 5 and naming it Ed's Grove.

Postcard view, circa 1954. While the words say "East Waterboro," Ed's was actually where Routes 4, 5, and 202 come together just over the Waterboro line in Lyman.

141

Postcard view, circa 1955. Since its days as Ken's Seafood Place the structure shown here has seen service as a grocery store, then was vacant, then as a knick knack shop, and is now (as of October 2001) vacant again.

KEN'S SEAFOOD PLACE
VERONA ISLAND

"It was a dine and dance place. He had a restaurant and sold all kinds of seafood. Had takeout, too. There was also a jukebox and a small dance area." So recalls Verona resident and selectman, Lloyd Bridges, 71.

Ken's, owned and operated by one Ken Cromwell, opened in 1952 and closed circa 1958. In between there was, per Lloyd, good food and good times, with dancing in the front and eats in the back. Or at least that's the way Lloyd recollects that it was. "That's about all I can recall," he chuckles. "I was more interested in girls then."

Fried Clams

NEW MEADOWS LOBSTER POUND/INN
WEST BATH

The New Meadows goes back to 1898. But in name and location only. The original New Meadows Inn burned to the ground in May of 1937. Constructed in 1898, the New Meadows opened for business on January 9, 1899. According to William C. Purington in his 1976 book, A LOOK INTO WEST BATH'S PAST, fried clams (as well as lobster stew, steamed clams, sweet doughnuts, and other goodies) were on the Inn's menu. Sundays, again according to Mr. Purington, often saw 800-900 people trying their darnedest to get in the Inn.

Long lines were not unusual.

After the fire, the Inn's old location sat vacant for a year or two before being re-opened as a lobster pound, under the direction of Samuel L. Armstrong. Armstrong, who'd purchased the property and the rights to the New Meadows' name from initial proprietor Charles H. Cahill, built on the installment plan. He affixed an addition here; another there. The present eatery is the sum of the structure shown here plus the various additions (including a banquet/meeting room tacked on in 1969).

Postcard view, circa 1948. The "new" New Meadows in its younger, "slimmer," and, in my opinion, better-looking days. Note the strong Howard Johnson influence.

Postcard view,
circa 1940.

SURF-SIDE LUNCH
YORK BEACH

I like the Surf-Side because it looks like a diner and I like diners. It was most likely built in the 1930s by a family named Roberge, and occupied a site that had previously been home to the York Public Bath House. For 40 or so years it satisfied summer hunger with hamburgers, hot dogs, ice cream, "special dinners," and, of course, fried clams. The original Surf-Side - the one pictured here - was demolished in 1974 to make way for a complex that today includes a newer and much larger Surf-Side, a candlepin bowling and game arcade, and Joan's Beach and Gift Shop.

P.S. On the message side of this postcard, postmarked July 3, 1941 and sent from "Mom" to "Dad" back home in Syracuse, there is the notation "Don't Lose This Card." So far nobody has.

Fried Clams

LEDGE WOOD RESTAURANT NORTH KENNEBUNKPORT (NOW ARUNDEL)

Ruth Weiss, 67, smiled a big smile when I showed her this postcard view. It seems she worked at Ledge Wood as a waitress in 1963-1964. "It was old-fashioned and cozy," she recalls. "They'd have a nice fireplace going. It was always busy." Ruth also readily recalls the tips and that she'd average $25.00-$30.00 a day, not at all bad for those times. Plus she could eat all she wanted. Ruth's favorite, alas, was not the Ledge Wood's noteworthy fried clams. No, Ruth liked the spaghetti, and veal cutlet. Not so

with her husband Richard, though. "On days off we'd go down (to the Ledge Wood) and my husband would eat fried clams. That's all he would eat."

The building you see here, situated at 2365 Portland Road/Route 1, ceased being a restaurant in 1976. It then served, until late 1998, as an Eagles Club. It is now, considerably the worse for the wear, a private residence.

Ad, Kennebunkport Playhouse program, August 1948.

ENJOY FINE FOOD IN AN UNIQUE ATMOSPHERE AT
The LEDGE WOOD RESTAURANT
"With the Rustic Dining Room"
STEAKS AND CHOPS, LOBSTER, FRIED CLAMS, SALADS
Tasty Sandwiches and Regular Dinners
SPECIAL MENU DAILY
-- Visit Our New Gift and Souvenir Shop --
Route 1, North Kennebunkport — 2 Miles South of Biddeford

Postcard view, circa 1936. Ledge Wood opened in 1933. Here's how it looked in its early years when original proprietor Ralph Sanborn was owner/operator.

SPILLER'S
YORK BEACH

Spiller's was a fixture in York Beach for 46 years. It was begun in late 1937 when restaurant veteran Alpheus Spiller and his wife, Nina Tapley Spiller, bought what had been a residence facing the ocean at Short Sands Beach. By the summer of '38 they had transformed their purchase into a take-out eatery. Specialities were fried clams, French fried potatoes, and homemade potato chips. Hamburgers and hot dogs soon followed. In 1940 Alpheus and Nina added a soda fountain and a few tables and converted their endeavor into a milk bar. The next step, after the war, was to enlarge their operation into a small - but full-scale - restaurant. This did so well that in 1950 the couple added a second story and created a formal dining room.

Alpheus and Nina's son Dexter and daughter-in-law Virginia took over in 1964-1965 and ran Spiller's until 1984. By then, recalls Dexter, good help was "getting scarce" and the 18-hour days weren't as much fun as they had been. Since 1984 the structure, located at 17 Ocean Avenue, has served as a convenience store and laundromat downstairs and a bar and restaurant upstairs. But to many it will always be Spiller's. And fried clams. "It's (the clams) what people remember," smiles Dexter.

P.S. There was also a Spiller's Inn, a more formal establishment owned by the Spillers, in operation on Route 1 until 1946. On that site there is now the Cape Neddick Inn.

Fried Clams

Ocean Avenue, York Beach, Me.

Postcard view, circa 1940. This shot was prior to the second story addition, and the hip roof from when the structure had been a residence is clearly visible in the background. After 1950 it would not be.

MAINE

The way FRIED CLAMS should be

R. HUBSCH

THE GREAT FRIED CLAM TASTE-OFF

Unlike dance halls and drive-in theatres, there are undoubtedly more fried clam establishments in Maine now than in the past. How many such establishments are there? Two hundred? Three hundred? Let's just say there are a lot. For both the fun of it and the taste of it my wife Catherine and I decided to do a little investigating. Our goal, starting with recommendations from friends, neighbors, town officials, and other usually reliable sources, was to establish a solid two dozen of the very best when it comes to frying up those tasty morsels. A secondary goal

was to not just "cover" the coastline. Here we did quite well: Auburn, Augusta, Emery Mills, Lincoln, and Newport will likely never have to worry about beach erosion.

The Findings

Our taste-off results, in alphabetical order, follow over the next eight pages. Before you immerse yourself in them too seriously, however, it should be made clear that our findings are far from scientific or final. On a different day we might well have come up with quite different

Fried Clams

opinions. Also, it should be noted that Catherine did 95% of the taste-testing. A native Mainer, she's been partaking of fried clams almost since solid food superceded Gerber's in her diet. I, on the other hand, am merely a novice. Enjoy the ratings and the write-ups. Better yet, enjoy some Maine fried clams.

P.S. There were many other clam-spot recommendations that we simply did not get to visit. There were, after all, just so many fried clams even in our Fried Clam Summer of 2001. These other recommendations include: Captain Newick's (South Portland); Five Islands Lobster Co. (Five Islands); the Helm (Rockport): Huoy's (Cape Ellis); the Lively Lobster (Old Orchard Beach); Lobster Pot (Cape Porpoise); Lobster Pound (Lincolnville Beach); Maxwell's (Bath); the Seafood Center (Arundel); Susan's Fish & Chips (Portland). I strongly suspect there are many other good places out there, too. How many fried clam eateries are there in Maine? A lot.

... at Bob's Clam Hut.

Catherine on the job...

... at Jake's.

Bob's Clam Hut
197 U.S. Route 1
Kittery
439-4919

It's difficult to find much to like about the Kittery Strip, but Bob's comes through. Opened in 1956, it is a pleasant throwback to the past.

TASTE: Good, but not as crispy as we would have liked.
VALUE: Too few clams for the dollar.
OUTSIDE: Attractive, with a plentiful supply of picnic tables.
INSIDE: Large and attractive dining area complete with curtains.

The Clam Shack
2 Western
Avenue/Route 9
Kennebunk
967-2560

At 12' wide by 8' deep, the Clam Shack is small in size. But it's big on clams. Just don't try to find a parking spot.

TASTE: Crispy and with good bellies but only so-so on flavor.
VALUE: No bargain here: cost per clam is high.
OUTSIDE: Standing room only, but there's a view of the Kennebunk River and the crowds that mill here and there and everwhere.
INSIDE: You'd have to be kidding!

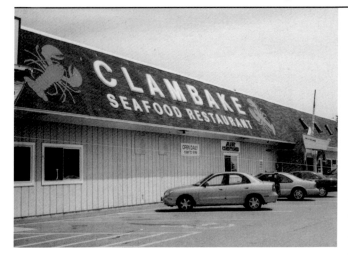

The Clambake
Route 9
Pine Point,
Scarborough
883-4871

The Clambake, in operation since 1987, is one of several eateries that carry on the tradition of Pine Point and clams. And it does so in a *big* way: the Clambake seats over 700.

TASTE: Nice and chewy, with a flavor that would rank "9" on a scale of 1 to 10.
VALUE: Average.
OUTSIDE: No outside seating.
INSIDE: Four huge dining rooms.

Fried Clams

Crosby's Drive-In
Lower Main
Street/Route 46
Bucksport
469-3640

Named after its original owner, one "Fats" Crosby, Crosby's goes back a good 50-60 years. A gem is its original neon tubing that spells out "Hot Dogs," "Lobster Rolls," and, of course, "Fried Clams."

TASTE: Crunchy and flavorful coating but too many pieces/not enough full clams.
VALUE: Average.
OUTSIDE: Two picnic table areas, one under the cover of a wooden roof.
INSIDE: No inside seating.

Dave's Restaurant
190 New County
Rd./Route 1
Thomaston
594-5424

Family owned, Dave's is locally popular and would seem to be a special favorite of the older crowd. Located north of Thomaston center on the Rockland line.

TASTE: Heavy dosage of crumbs, almost as if the clams were in batter. Nice flavor, but could have been crispier.
VALUE: Average.
OUTSIDE: No outside seating.
INSIDE: Attractive large dining room featuring a long counter and stools.

Harmon's Fried
Clams
Headquartered in
Windsor
549-3346

Founded as Canora's in Higgins Beach in 1949, Harmon's is today a much-heralded traveling clam shack road show, setting up at the Windsor, Farmington, and Fryeburg fairs.

TASTE: Not as many bellies as we might have liked, but pieces galore, each in a tasty and crunchy batter.
VALUE: Good value.
OUTSIDE: Varies by fair but you may be certain there'll be a goodly share of picnic tables.
INSIDE: No inside seating.

Harraseeket Lunch
Maine Street
South Freeport
865-4888

Harraseeket's is set amidst a working - and picturesque! - waterfront. Popular with tourists.

TASTE: Very tasty with lots of batter. (Crumbs are available, too). Nice crunchiness.
VALUE: Poor value: chances are you won't come away feeling stuffed to the gills.
OUTSIDE: Numerous picnic tables, all with a view of water or boats or both.
INSIDE: Attractive dining room with a neat and nautical feel.

Holbrook's Lobster Wharf
Cundy's Harbor
725-0708

Holbrook's would have to be near the top of any chart that measured beauteous water views. We did, however, find the service to be uncommonly slow.

TASTE: Full-bellied, well-flavored, and juicy.
VALUE: Not a good value.
OUTSIDE: Lots of seating, all with that great water view.
INSIDE: None, although there is a substantial overhang that covers a large portion of the outdoor seating.

Jake's Seafood
Route 1
Moody
646-6771

We came upon Jake's early in our research process and were so enamored of its clams that all subsequent candidates were measured against it. None ever topped it.

TASTE: Nice and chewy in a crispy and mouth-watering batter. And fried in cholesterol-free canola oil, too.
VALUE: Average.
OUTSIDE: Attractive and comfy - although somewhat in need of paint in places - picnic table area.
INSIDE: Smallish but attractive dining room.

Fried Clams

Kate's Seafood
1606 U.S. Route 1
Rockland
594-2626

Kate's is *very* attractive, featuring grey shakes and red and white trim. We were, however, disappointed in our primary reason for being there: the clams.

TASTE: Fairly flavorful, but overly greasy. Made us want to dip the clams in tartar sauce.
VALUE: Average.
OUTSIDE: No outdoor tables or benches. We sat on the side lawn.
INSIDE: A sizable dining room that, in keeping with Kate's exterior, is most attractive.

Lisa's Lobster
Moore's Turnpike Rd.
Five Islands,
Georgetown
371-2722

As hinted by the homemade sign pictured here, finding Lisa's is no easy trick. The food and the view, though, make the hunt worthwhile.

TASTE: Very greasy but with good flavor. Salty.
VALUE: Average.
OUTSIDE: Five scattered picnic tables, each with a bedazzling water view.
INSIDE: No indoor seating.

The Log Cabin
Route 2, East
Newport
368-4551

Although well off the Clam Trail, the Log Cabin serves up a deserving product from a good-looking built-in-1947 log-cabin-like structure.

TASTE: Nicely full-bellied but a bit too soggy and possessing a rather bland crumb flavor.
VALUE: Lotta clams for your money.
OUTSIDE: No outside tables or benches.
INSIDE: Three very nicely appointed dining rooms with dark wood and green and white trim.

Maine Diner
Route 1
Wells
646-4442

A Maine favorite and seemingly always packed, the Maine Diner *could* well serve more meals per year than any other non-chain eating establishment in the state.

TASTE: High in flavor but could be a little crispier.
VALUE: Not a bargain.
OUTSIDE: There is no outside eating area.
INSIDE: An all-stool counter plus two pleasing dining areas and a plentitude of framed reviews, photos, etc. that adds sparkle.

Moody's Diner
Route 1
Waldoboro
832-7785

With roots that stretch back to 1927, Moody's is more than a restaurant. It is a legend. And (see Maine Diner, above) it is Moody's that *may* well serve the most meals per year.

TASTE: Nicely crispy/crunchy but a mite lacking in flavor.
VALUE: Good value.
OUTSIDE: No outside eating area.
INSIDE: You feel as if you're in a wonderful old friend of a diner. And you are.

Red Barn
Riverside Drive
Route 201
Augusta
523-9485

It was not love at first bite at this brightly-painted eatery on Route 201 north of town. We blamed it on a high grease factor.

TASTE: After a disappointing start we found that we began to really enjoy the clams, their crumb batter, their flavor.
VALUE: Average.
OUTSIDE: Nicely maintained and colorful picnic table area.
INSIDE: Small but comely dining room.

Fried Clams

Red's Eats
Water & Main
Sts./Route 1
Wiscasset
882-6128

A Route 1 landmark since 1938, Red's is probably Maine's consummate road-side take-out restaurant. You want eats? Red's has eats.

TASTE: Fine-flavored batter; crispy and chewy, too. Rates an 8 on a scale of 1 to 10.
VALUE: Average.
OUTSIDE: Backyard picnic table patio with a view of the Sheepscot River and Route 1 traffic.
INSIDE: Red's is much too small for any inside seating.

Richard's Seafood
Route 9, West
Wells
646-8561

Don't look for a water view at Richard's. Although located in Wells, it's well-removed from the ocean on the road to North Berwick.

TASTE: Nice flavor; chewy; lots of bellies. Greasy but good grease. Right up there with the best.
VALUE: Very good: you won't go hungry at Richard's.
OUTSIDE: Attractively-landscaped picnic table area.
INSIDE: Neat and nautical, but somewhat bland, dining area.

Sail Inn
Route 1
Prospect
469-3850

There's clams and there's clams with a view. The Sail Inn is very definitely the latter. Its Penobscot River/Waldo-Hancock Bridge vista is nothing short of breathtaking.

TASTE: Nice and chewy and juicy: there's a lot to like about the Sail Inn's clams.
VALUE: Average.
OUTSIDE: You may be so taken with the view from the deck you forget to fully appreciate the clams.
INSIDE: Same view from an open and airy dining room.

155

Sea Basket
Route 1
Wiscasset
882-6581

Since it opened in 1981 the Sea Basket has been known for its fried seafood. Their clams do not disappoint: they're right up there with the best.

TASTE: Appeared to be fried in almost a cross between crumbs and batter. Nice flavor. Good bellies.
VALUE: Good value.
OUTSIDE: Small but attractive picnic area.
INSIDE: Three small dining rooms; bright and cheery and highlighted by a pair of handsome seascape wall murals.

Snack Shack
Route 2
Lincoln
794-6565

Visualize this photo in bright red and white and you visualize the Snack Shack. It has a happy face!

TASTE: Lincoln's contribution to Fried Clamland features a batter that's light and nicely flavored.
VALUE: Not a great value.
OUTSIDE: Grab a picnic table if you can: there are but two of them.
INSIDE: No indoor seating.

Tall Barney's
Main Street
Jonesport
497-2403

Named in honor of a local gentle giant of a man called Barnabas B. Beal, Tall Barney's is a downeast fried clam stronghold.

TASTE: Good and chewy but not as much full-bellied flavor as we would have liked.
VALUE: Average.
OUTSIDE: A pair of well-seasoned picnic tables and a view of what's happening on Main Street.
INSIDE: Two comfortable - but unexciting - dining rooms.

Fried Clams

Two Lights Lobster Shack
225 Two Lights Rd.
Cape Elizabeth
799-1677

As with a hefty number of our picks, you are apt to venture to Two Lights as much for the view as for the food. It would be difficult to go amiss with either.

TASTE: High in flavor and very high in crunch (too high for Catherine; just right for me).
VALUE: Not as good as the view.
OUTSIDE: An abundance of picnic tables spread out, almost literally, on a chunk of Maine's rocky coast.
INSIDE: Small, quaintly-decorated dining area.

Ted's Fried Clams
Route 109
Emery Mills
No telephone listed

Ted's is actually Ted's III. Begun in 1950 by Theodore Mavrakos, it has progressed - in size if not in beauty - from a tiny structure to its present sizable abode.

TASTE: One of our favorites: flavorful cornmeal batter; fine blend of chewy/crispy clams.
VALUE: Good value for the money.
OUTSIDE: Appealing picnic table area with ten all-in-a-row tables under a canvas canopy.
INSIDE: Large dining area featuring a separate "chowder bar."

Village Inn
165 High Street
Auburn
782-7796

Begun as Eddy's Diner circa 1934, the Village Inn (which also has a location in Old Orchard Beach) is justly renowned for good food and lots of it.

TASTE: The Village offers clams in both crumbs and batter. We opted for batter and found it almost irresistably good.
VALUE: No portion control here: our serving was *huge*.
OUTSIDE: No outside facilities.
INSIDE: Large and attractive dining area.

YARMOUTH CLAM FESTIVAL
YARMOUTH

No account of fried clams in Maine - or the rest of the country or elsewhere, for that matter - would be complete without the inclusion of the Yarmouth Clam Festival. With a convoluted history that goes back to the 1930s, the Festival has grown - and grown, and grown - to herculean proportions. When we turned out for the three-day event in July 2001 we were but two of an estimated crowd of 150,000 fun and food seekers. I don't know about the estimated other 149,998, but we had ourselves a fine old time.

Photo, July 21, 2001. Main Street becomes Clam Festival Street every July in Yarmouth.

Fried Clams

Photos, both July 21, 2001. The lines were lengthy but worth the wait. In addition to fried clams in crumbs there was fried

clams in batter, clam chowder, stuffed clams, and clam cakes. It was enough to make most anyone happy as a _____.

Included here, to add some zing to a section that might otherwise be considered ho hum, are a number of reduced-size vintage postcards. Known as "comic cards," they will probably not cause you to split your sides. But they may cause you to smile.

AH! IT'S GOOD TO BE BACK IN

Houlton, Me.

8815

Index

A ticket to KISSMEQUICK R.R. TRUE LOVE LINE ONE FIRST CLASS PASSAGE TO Bangor, Maine Dan Cupid GENERAL PASSENGER AGENT 4-14- is a sure guide to Heaven!

Index